THE CONFLICT IN EDUCATION

THE CONFLICT
IN EDUCATION

In a Democratic Society

By

ROBERT M. HUTCHINS

GREENWOOD PRESS, PUBLISHERS
WESTPORT, CONNECTICUT

The Library of Congress has catalogued this publication as follows:

Library of Congress Cataloging in Publication Data

Hutchins, Robert Maynard, 1899-
   The conflict in education in a democratic society.

   1. Education--Philosophy. 2. Education--U. S.
I. Title.
[LB875.H96 1972]   370.1   77-138117
ISBN 0-8371-5693-9

Originally published in 1953 by Harper & Row Publishers,
Inc.

Reprinted with the permission of Harper & Row Publishers,
Inc.

Reprinted in 1972 by Greenwood Press,
A division of Congressional Information Service, Inc.
88 Post Road West, Westport, Connecticut 06881

Library of Congress catalog card number 77-138117
ISBN 0-8371-5693-9

Printed in the United States of America

10 9 8 7 6 5 4 3

CONTENTS

PREFACE

This book is based on the Gottesman Lectures delivered at the University of Uppsala in 1951 and the Marfleet Lectures given at the University of Toronto in 1952. I am grateful to the authorities of these institutions for permission to publish these materials in this volume.

R. M. H.

Pasadena, California
February 2, 1953

THE CONFLICT IN EDUCATION

CHAPTER I

ADJUSTMENT TO THE ENVIRONMENT

THIS book deals with the philosophy of education. I hope to show that the philosophy of education, by which I mean a reasoned and coherent statement of its aims and possibilities, is a secondary subject, dependent on our conception of man and society, that is, upon our philosophy in general. I shall suggest that the chaos now obtaining in the philosophy of education results from the chaos in philosophy in general.

For this purpose we shall first go through the prevailing theories or doctrines of education, indicating the consequences that each has had, or is likely to have, upon the progress of mankind. These theories or doctrines I take to be the doctrine of adaptation or adjustment; the doctrine of immediate needs, or what might be called the doctrine of the *ad hoc*; the doctrine of social reform; and the doctrine that we need no doctrine at all. I shall then attempt to outline a doctrine that seems, because it is based upon a sounder philosophy in general, to offer more hope as a philosophy of education.

The examples I shall use are largely American. The

principal reason for this is, of course, that I have
spent thirty years as a teacher and administrator in
American educational institutions. But there are other
reasons, too. America is a sign and a portent. American technology, which has been a most significant
force in moulding American society, seems destined
to extend throughout the world. America was the first
country to try to educate a whole population, and, as
other countries take up this program, as they seem
sure to do, they are likely to encounter some of the
same problems with which America is now wrestling.
America has suddenly emerged as the richest and
most powerful nation in the world. Since every nation
wants to be rich and powerful, it is possible—there
are signs of this already—that many will feel that one
way to become rich and powerful is to imitate the
American educational system. It may be useful to
raise the question whether America has become rich
and powerful because of her educational system or in
spite of it. Finally, the decay of philosophy has taken
place on a world-wide scale; but the effects of this
decay on education have for many reasons been more
immediate and more pronounced in America than
anywhere else. By observing the effects of the decay
of philosophy on education in America, the European
may, perhaps, learn what is in store for education
throughout the world.

Every ambition, at least every formal, material, institutional ambition, of the reformers, philanthropists,

and optimists of the nineteenth century has now been achieved. They wanted to end slavery, lengthen life, raise the standard of living, establish universal free education, and create one world. Science and technology were to be the principal instruments by which happiness and prosperity were to be forged. Science and technology have performed nobly. But the optimism is gone.

Thirty-five years ago we could sing with Shelley:

> The world's great age begins anew,
> The golden years return,
> And earth doth like a snake renew
> Her winter weeds outworn:
> Heaven smiles, and faiths and empires gleam,
> Like wrecks of a dissolving dream.

Now we question whether legal slavery is the only slavery there is, whether a longer life is necessarily a a good thing if that life is aimless, whether improvement in the material conditions of existence can solve the fundamental problems of existence, whether one bad world may not be worse than many, and whether science and technology can give us the wisdom to use the power they have brought us for the benefit rather than the destruction of mankind. We question particularly whether universal compulsory free education is, as we always supposed it was, a sufficient method of dealing with all the issues raised by freeing the slaves, giving everybody the vote, and developing industrialism.

The Enlightenment based its hopes of progress on

the spread of universal education; and one of its children, Edward Gibbon, in his celebrated chapter summarizing the reasons for the fall of the Western Empire, relieves the fears of Europe by saying that there never will be another barbarian conqueror. His reason is simple. War now requires the knowledge of a large number of arts and sciences. Hence to excel in war the barbarian must cease to be barbarous. Since man first discovered how to master the forces of nature all history has been tending toward this goal. Gibbon's final remark is, "We may therefore acquiesce in the pleasing conclusion that every age of the world has increased and still increases the real wealth, the happiness, the knowledge, and perhaps the virtue of the human race."

The conclusion is pleasing, but seems to be false. There is evidence that the rate of increase in real wealth is declining and none that the happiness and virtue of the human race are increasing. And we know now that a conqueror equipped with knowledge can be more barbarous, as well as more dangerous, than any of his unlettered predecessors.

As for those expectations of political equality and justice which were founded on universal education, Aldous Huxley could say not long ago, "But in actual historical fact, the spread of free compulsory education, and, along with it, the cheapening and acceleration of the older methods of printing, have almost everywhere been followed by an increase in the power of ruling oligarchies at the expense of the masses."

This proposition, if true, is certainly one of the most sensational paradoxes in human history. The sensation is in the fact that it was totally unforeseen. For two hundred years proposals to broaden the suffrage have uniformly been accompanied by proposals to broaden education. Those who have wanted political power for the masses and those who have opposed political power for them have always agreed in this, that, if they were to have political power, they must have education. Huxley finds that, as they have got education, their political power has diminished instead of increasing.

Arnold Toynbee discovers the explanation for the failure of universal education in the rise of what are called the media of mass communication. He says, "The bread of universal education is no sooner cast upon the waters of social life than a shoal of sharks rises from the depths and devours the children's bread before the philanthropists' eyes. In the educational history of England, for example, the dates speak for themselves. Universal compulsory gratuitous education was inaugurated in this country in A.D. 1870; the Yellow Press was invented some twenty years later—as soon as the first generation of children from the national schools came into the labor market and acquired some purchasing power —by a stroke of irresponsible genius which had divined that the educational philanthropists' labor of love could be made to yield the newspaper king a royal profit."

Mr. Toynbee even goes so far as to imply that the totalitarian state is a reaction against what he calls "the enormity of the Yellow Press—and of other instruments, like the Cinema, that have since been invented for the same lucrative business of making a profit out of the entertainment of the masses." He naturally finds this remedy worse than the disease. His conclusion is: "Thus in countries where the system of Universal Education has been introduced, the people are in danger of falling under an intellectual tyranny of one kind or another, whether it be exercised by private capitalists or public authorities."

Mr. Toynbee has a remedy to propose. He says that the only course open to us in the fight against intellectual tyranny is "to raise the level of mass cultivation to a degree at which the minds of the children who are put through the educational mill are rendered immune against at least the grosser forms of either private or public propaganda."

Mr. Toynbee's remedy is singularly like that offered by Victor Ratner, once vice-president of the Columbia Broadcasting System, who says, "Radio is made in the image of the American people. To lambaste it is itself un-American. The critics hit at it because they claim to be shocked at what the United States' people are. Radio fits the people. The masses like comic books, Betty Grable, broad comedy, simple drama—it's vulgar, fast, simple, fundamental. Critics of radio often speak about the people's fare; yet they seem to refuse to face the facts about the people's taste. Such criticisms are really criticisms of the American educational system for not raising the cultural level of Americans; for not getting them interested in the better things when they are young. Radio then gets the blame for this failure."

The proposal is to remake the public, to fend off the influences of the media of mass communication, by raising the level of mass cultivation through the system of universal compulsory education.

This leads first to the very large question whether and to what extent the state of mind of the public is or can be the result of its educational system. Universal free compulsory education would seem to be a reflection of what the country wants. One of the most important ideas about education is compressed into the Platonic line: "What is honored in a country will be cultivated there." This is true at the highest levels, in determining the course of research and advanced study. The interest in science and technology in the United States today must result from the honor in which scientists and technologists are held and from the high value that is set upon their work. It is even truer at the level of universal compulsory education, because the object of the system must be to make the children as far as possible what their parents or the

ruling group in the community want the next generation to be. This is what will be honored in the country. It does not seem an exaggeration to say that a
system of universal free compulsory education, however expensive or prolonged, can do no more than
try to give the people what they want already. It cannot make them want something different. If the
American people honored wisdom and goodness as
they now honor power and success, the system of
universal free education would be quite different
from what it is today. But how can the system of
universal free education, which is busily cultivating
what the people now honor, teach them to honor
something else?

This would seem to be sufficient answer to Mr.
Ratner, and it may even be a sufficient comment on
Mr. Toynbee. But there are other answers, too. As
the arrangements in other parts of the world show,
there is no inherent reason why the American radio
should be conducted for profit; and there is no reason
why it should be conducted as it is, even if it is conducted for profit. To give all the best time to vaude-
ville and all the rest to soap opera is a crime for
which the fine music that comes occasionally over the
air cannot atone. Why should Mr. Ratner demand
that the educational system do for him something he
could at least in part achieve himself? A man who
has a monopoly, and then sells shoddy merchandise,
can hardly blame the low taste of the public or the

ineffectiveness of its educational system for his prosperity. The public has nowhere to turn. Mr. Ratner
has no monopoly; but he and his colleagues in other
broadcasting companies are so busy imitating one another that what the listener finds on one station he
will find on another; and, if he does not like what
he finds, he must turn his radio off altogether.

The final answer to Mr. Toynbee and Mr. Ratner
is that from the point of view of time alone they have
proposed an undue burden on the schools. As Alfred
North Whitehead remarked, "The whole problem of
education is controlled by lack of time. If Methuselah
was not educated, it was his own fault or that of his
teachers." A child is in school for only a small por-
tion of his life, and even when he is of school age he
is not protected, after hours, from the terrific storm
of propaganda that now beats upon the citizen. The
notion that the child can be inoculated against propaganda once and for all in childhood seems naïve. It
is hardly possible that this task can be accomplished
for life in eight, twelve, or sixteen years.

Nevertheless we must admit that Mr. Toynbee is
on the right track, even if his track is not long enough
to carry us to our destination. He suggests, in his talk
of raising the level of mass cultivation, the reason
why universal education has failed to achieve the intellectual, social, and political results expected of it
and has, in fact, produced results exactly opposite to
those which were confidently hoped for. It cannot be

said that the sort of popular education now prevalent in America, and destined, I believe, to spread over the West, has raised the level of mass cultivation, or has been engaged in cultivation of any kind.

How do you get a country to want to raise the level of mass cultivation? This depends on criticism, criticism by individuals, minorities, and centers of independent thought. This is the reason for academic freedom and freedom of speech generally. The best definition of a university that I have been able to think of is that it is a center of independent thought. It may be a good many other things as well; but, if it is not this, it has failed. The principal function of a professional school in a university is not to train men for the profession, but to criticize the profession. Unless criticism of the culture is permitted, the culture cannot be changed; certainly the schools will not be permitted to change it.

How do you get a country to permit criticism? This can only be done if the country recognizes that an uncriticized culture cannot long endure. The hope of the West is that the church and the university are still free. I must add that there is no hope in the university unless it takes seriously its mission as a center of independent thought.

Any opinion that a man holds simply because it has been pumped or pounded into him is no good, because it cannot last. Children should be brought up in good habits; but those habits cannot endure the stress and strain of circumstances unless they have some foundation in the convictions of the person who has them. Durable conviction about the affairs of this world is a matter of reason. It is easy to show by reason that Marxism is a fallacious doctrine. But what if the person with whom you are discussing it has never learned to reason? Since we cannot hope to insulate our young people from access to the false doctrines in the world, the thing to do is to train them so that they can see the falsity in them. This means helping them learn to think for themselves.

Am I saying that the public should not control the educational system? Certainly not. I am saying that the public should understand education. And it would do no harm if teachers and professors understood it, too. Indoctrination and propaganda have no place in it. The private opinions of teachers are not to be pumped or pounded into young people any more than the majority opinion is. But in my observation, which covers a very long period, there is not much danger to our youth from the improprieties of their instructors or the radical views that they may entertain. I am sure that 75 per cent of the professors at the University of Chicago voted for Landon. A far greater danger is that the majority will exert pressure on the educational system for indoctrination in and compulsory adoption of the majority opinion. The rule of the majority without free discussion and criticism is tyranny.

If the public, the teachers, and the professors all understood the educational system, we could develop a tradition in this country that would be far more effective in giving us the kind of education we need than laws, witch-hunts, or regulations that teachers must subscribe to oaths that, as Governor Warren of California has said, any traitor would take with a laugh. On the side of the teachers and professors, the professional tradition would mean that they taught responsibly. On the side of the public the tradition would mean that the public restrained itself in the exercise of its legal control.

Because I am concerned with the development of this tradition I deplore every futile, childish, and irrelevant activity in which the educational system engages. Educators do things that the public wants in order to get the support of the public. They do little to explain to the public why it should not want the things it does. I like intercollegiate football, but I recommended its abolition at Chicago, because the game in its industrial, big-time form has nothing to do with education and yet has the effect of diverting everybody's attention from the educational problems with which universities should be wrestling. So I deplore the multiplication of trivial courses, in cosmetology, fishing, and tapdancing, which swell the catalogues of great American universities and which have no purpose except to help the student wile away four years without using his mind. Think of

the most futile, childish, irrelevant subject you can—
think of parlor games, think of self-beautification,
think of anything you like—I will undertake to find
it for you among the courses offered by American institutions of higher learning.

I had no sooner written these words than *Life*
magazine came along to prove my point by announcing that at an American university it is possible to get
college credit for being a clown, something that even
I, after decades of disillusionment, could never have
thought of. *Life* concludes its account with words
that might well be the epitaph of the higher learning
in America: the students, says *Life*, regard this work
"as just part of a normal liberal education." I need say
no more to show that neither the public nor the educational profession has a clear conception of education. They have no standard by which to judge what
belongs in education and what does not.

What belongs in education is what helps the
student to learn to think for himself, to form an independent judgment, and to take his part as a responsible citizen. Although I will admit that in the
hands of Socrates any subject can be made important, even clowning, because any subject can lead to
important questions, there was only one Socrates, and
I know of none in any educational system today.
We have to frame the course of study of American
schools, colleges, and universities in the light of the
capacity of ordinary teachers. If the object of the

educational system is to help young people learn to think for themselves, it should help them to think about the most important subjects, and these are discussed in the greatest works of the greatest writers of the past and present. To destroy the Western tradition of independent thought it is not necessary to burn the books. All we have to do is to leave them unread for a couple of generations.

In the United States little effort is made to raise the level of mass cultivation through the schools. The leading theories or doctrines of education say nothing on this subject.

The first of these doctrines is the theory of adjustment. Here the object is to fit the student into his physical, social, political, economic, and intellectual environment with a minimum of discomfort to the society. Freud took the view that the object of education was to make young people healthy and efficient, to adapt them to their surroundings, to make them successful in the terms of the society in which they were brought up. His summary is: "I should go so far as to say that revolutionary children are not desirable from any point of view." This caution seems unnecessary; for no society would tolerate a revolutionary educational system.

So T. S. Eliot seems to give his powerful sanction to an educational program that adapts the child to the political organization under which he is to live.

So the chief aim of the program of UNESCO in

fundamental education, which is the principal program of the organization, is to enable the peoples of underdeveloped countries "to adjust themselves to their changing environment."

In America the doctrine of adjustment is perhaps the leading theory. Here it results from a misconception of John Dewey. Since he is not a clear writer, his followers may perhaps be excused for their failure to notice that when he talked about adjustment to the environment, he meant that the environment should first be improved. Dewey was essentially a social reformer, and it is tragic that he should have laid the foundation for the proposition that the aim of education is to adjust the young to their environment, good or bad.

The theory of adjustment or adaptation was carried to its logical extreme in a women's college in America, which based its curriculum on a job analysis of the diaries of 323 mature women. The categories of the activities of these women constitute the structure of the curriculum, without regard to whether or not mature women ought to do or are now doing the things that 323 of them were doing when this poll was taken.

Thus it will be seen that the theory of adjustment leads to a curriculum of miscellaneous dead facts. The way to adjust to the environment is to learn the facts about the environment. Since it is impossible to tell what the environment will be, the student can only be informed about the environment that exists while he is in school. But all that is known with certainty about the environment is that it will be different by the time the student has to adjust himself to it.

The doctrine of adjustment or adaptation is not well adapted to America. America is, and always has been, a society in transition. Seventy million Americans live in a different house today from the one they occupied ten years ago. America is the example par excellence of the rapidity of technological change. Vocations employing thousands of men may be wiped out overnight and be replaced by others that were not thought of the day before.

One of the most popular courses in the American schools is stenography. Think of the havoc that will be wrought if the dictating machine becomes the standard method of conducting office correspondence. A great American university has established a school of what is called cosmetology, announcing that what it called the profession of beautician "is the fastest growing in this state." Think what will happen to the graduates of this educational institution if self-beautification for ladies becomes as simple a matter as it is for men.

America is probably the easiest place to earn a living in the world. Yet more emphasis is placed on vocational training in the American schools than in any others. There are many reasons for this; but the one I wish to mention now is an example of the proposition that what is honored in a country will be cultivated there. We must admit that what is honored in America is material success. All you have to do to understand this is to compare the position of intellectuals and artists in America with their position in Europe. The model American is the successful businessman. Artists and intellectuals are regarded in the light of charity patients or excess baggage. Consequently the attention of the American is drawn at an early date to the necessity of adjusting himself to his economic environment in such a way that he will be successful.

I shall attempt in a moment a general critique of the doctrine of adjustment or adaptation. Here I wish to mention one or two consequences of that branch of the doctrine which deals with economic or vocational adjustment. The question it raises is this: assuming that the young must adjust to their environment, including their economic environment, can the educational system manage, supervise, and direct the whole job? In particular, can the educational system give a boy as good a training for a particular task in industry as the industry itself could give him? In America technical institutes of the European type are virtually unknown. Vocational training is given along with all other types of training in the same schools. Because of the relative ease of vocational instruction and because of the immediate interest it excites on the part of the pupil, such instruction has the tendency to force out of the course of study any other kind of instruction. Yet we learned in the war that the airplane companies could produce in a few weeks better airplane mechanics than the schools could produce in years. The pupils in the schools were necessarily trained by obsolescent teachers with obsolescent machinery. Hence the result of the emphasis on vocational training in America is poor mechanics without education.

America is not only the easiest place to earn a living in the world; it is also the place with the most leisure in the world. The average industrial worker in America gets more than fifty dollars for a forty-hour week. He now works twenty hours a week less than he did forty years ago. At the same time that industrial operations have been simplified to the point where little or no training is required for them—they can in fact be performed by twelve-year-old children—unprecedented leisure has opened before the American citizen. Still one of the principal aims of the educational system is to educate the citizen to work for a living. It does not educate him at all in the right use of his leisure.

The new found leisure of the American is therefore spent in relaxation, and that provided by the tavern and the television set is almost equally demoralizing. The prospect that television opens before us in America, with nobody speaking and nobody reading, suggests that a bleak and torpid epoch may lie ahead in which the population will eventually sink, in accordance with the principles of evolution, to the level of the lowest forms of vegetable life.

Scientists of the University of Chicago have lately detected something that looks like moss growing on the planet Mars. Perhaps Mars was once inhabited by beings like ourselves, who had the misfortune, some millions of years ago, to invent television. The twin aims that have animated mankind since the dawn of history, the conquest of nature and relief from drudgery, now almost accomplished in America, have ended in the trivialization of our lives.

There are, of course, many reasons for this; but one of them surely is that our educational system has given us no resources that we can employ to give our leisure time significance. When we are not working, all we can do is to amuse ourselves. The deep and permanent melancholia that underlies the American temperament must be ascribed, in part at least, to the boredom that the perpetual search for amusement at length induces.

The whole doctrine of adjustment to the environment seems to me radically erroneous. As I have said, it leads to a curriculum of miscellaneous dead facts. It leads to vocational training, which the schools are not equipped to give and which misses the most important contribution that the schools can make. But it is far more urgent that we notice that our mission here on earth is to change our environment, not to adjust ourselves to it. If we become mal-adjusted in the process, so much the worse for the environment. The message that UNESCO should carry to the people of backward countries is not that they should adjust themselves to their changing environment, but that they should change their environment.

If we have to choose between Sancho Panza and Don Quixote, let us by all means choose Don Quixote. Or, to pass from models supplied by fiction to those offered us by real life, let us remember that Socrates and Gandhi did not seek to adapt themselves to society as they found it. They attempted to re-make society, and the fact that they died in the attempt in no way detracts from their glory or from their value as examples to other men. To Freud we may oppose Kant, who said, "Parents usually educate their children merely in such a manner that, however bad the world may be, they may adapt themselves to its present conditions." This may suggest to us that the doctrine of adaptation is not so new as its proponents would have us believe. Kant goes on: "But they ought to give them an education so much better than this, that a better condition of things may thereby be brought about in the future."

The pressure in America, especially intense now in this period of the cold war, is toward a flat conformity of life and thought. University professors are being required in some states to take special oaths attesting that they have never been members of the Communist party, and this in spite of the fact that, unless a recent ambiguous decision of the Supreme Court has changed the law, it is perfectly legal to be a Communist in the United States. The irresponsible fulminations of Senator McCarthy strike terror into the hearts of innocent government employees. Students who exhibit the slightest variation from established fashions of thought and action ask me whether they are neurotic. And, in fact, I attribute the popularity of psychoanalysis in the United States in large part to the prevailing impression that everybody who is not just like everybody else, or, worse still, who does not want to be, must be sick. The only serious doubt that one may have about democracy is whether it is possible to combine the rule of the majority with that independence of character, thought, and conduct which the progress of any society requires.

Against the tendency toward conformity the universities of America have been unable to fight effectively. One of the most interesting questions about university education in America is this: why is it that the boy who on June 15 receives his degree, eager, enthusiastic, outspoken, idealistic, reflective, and independent, is on the following September 15, or even on June 16, dull, uninspired, shifty, cautious, pliable, and attired in that symbol of respectability, worn by the vice-presidents of all banks, a double-breasted blue serge suit? Why are the graduates of the great American universities indistinguishable from the mass of the population who have never had their advantages? Why are the organized alumni of the country dedicated to the affectionate perpetuation of all the wrong things about their universities, such as intercollegiate football and drinking parties?

The answer lies in part where Mr. Toynbee found it, in the relative weakness of higher education compared with the forces that make everybody think and act like everybody else. Those forces beat upon the individual from birth on, almost twenty-four hours a day, and constitute an enormous obstacle to any educational effort. So much is this the case that it is now seriously argued in some quarters in America that, since education cannot compete with the comic book, it should absorb it and substitute elevating and instructive comic books for textbooks.

But the deeper answer is that everybody is supposed to be like everybody else. The doctrine of adaptation has won the day. A university that produced graduates who did not slide unobtrusively into the scenery would be accounted a failure, and perhaps a menace.

At least during a cold war, the doctrine of adaptation leads remorselessly to indoctrination. I will read you a few exemplary passages from a letter addressed to all the teachers in a Middle Western city by the superintendent of schools, who, under the law of the state, has the power to oust any of them from their jobs. The superintendent says, "The threat to American institutions by international communism makes imperative that greater emphasis be given in our schools to the study of the meaning, significance, and the value of American Democracy. Indoctrination has never been in good repute among educators in the United States. . . . It now appears necessary for the schools in the United States to indoctrinate American youth for American Democracy. . . . In our present confused world, it is essential in America that we teach our young people that American Democracy is the best government in the world and that we explain why it is the best. . . . They must understand that American Democracy was founded on private enterprise and that this economic system has brought forth a great and powerful nation which will continue to grow even stronger by perpetuating and protecting private enterprise." And so on.

Although I believe that democracy is the best form of government, that the American democracy is a very good form of democracy, and that the economic system known as private enterprise has made significant contributions to the development of my country, I ask myself whether it is possible for the American democracy to be improved and whether the American system of private enterprise has no defects, and also whether pupils who have been indoctrinated as this superintendent proposes can be expected to take an active part in improving the American government or remedying the defects of the American economic system. I also feel some sympathy for the confusion and disappointment that these pupils will experience when they emerge from the dream world of indoctrination and face the facts of life.

Here we see the doctrine of adaptation reduced to an absurdity; for the passion to adjust the young to the environment has so carried away this superintendent that in the name of adjustment he proposes to adjust the young, not to the environment, but to his conception of the environment, which can only result in maladjusting them to the environment as it actually is.

We hear during the cold war in America that the American way of life is in danger. You would suppose, to listen to the people who say this, that the American way of life consisted in unanimous tribal self-adoration. Yet the history and tradition of our country make it plain that the essence of the American way of life is its hospitality to criticism, protest, unpopular opinions, and independent thought. The great American word has always been freedom, and, in particular, freedom of thought, speech, and assembly. Asserting the dignity of man, and of every man, America has proclaimed and protected the freedom to differ. America has grown strong on criticism. It would be quite as consistent with the American way of life to offer prizes for the most penetrating criticism of our country as it would be to offer prizes to those who have done the best job of advertising it. The heart of democracy is independent criticism; the basic freedom is freedom of thought and expression.

Non-legal methods of persecuting people into conformity are steadily gaining popularity in the West. Such methods are little better than purges and pogroms. The ideas to which the West, and a large part of the East, are most bitterly opposed are the police state, the abolition of freedom of speech, thought, and association, and the notion that the individual exists for the state. Yet in practice there may not be a significant difference between a society in which such compulsions are exerted by the tyrannical power of the state and one in which they come from the tyrannical power of public opinion.

The doctrine of adjustment or adaptation explicitly excludes any consideration of standards. The adjustment must take place, whether the environment is good or bad. An educational system that is based on this theory must, therefore, ultimately become a system without values. I shall hope to show that an educational system without values is a contradiction in terms.

CHAPTER II

MEETING IMMEDIATE NEEDS

THE doctrine of immediate needs, or the doctrine of the *ad hoc*, looks, in terms of its practical results, a good deal like the doctrine of adaptation or adjustment to the environment. The course of study in the women's college that I described, where the curriculum is based on the diaries of 323 mature women, could be justified either on the ground that this program of study would adapt the graduates of the college to a society where mature women were behaving in this way or on the ground that young women needed to learn to behave in this way in order to behave like mature women.

Or take an announcement made not long ago in an educational journal in America on behalf of the high school of San Diego, California. It states that the high school has extended its requirements for graduation beyond the usual academic hurdles and now includes in these requirements what are called "Essentials for Effective Living." Among the essentials for effective living appear the following: ability to apply first aid; ability to take care of one's self in the water (we are reminded that San Diego is a seaport town); ability to engage in two or three sports that may carry over into adult life; ability to write business letters; ability to fill out application blanks; and ability to budget one's income. The girls have to acquire in addition ability to buy the right kind of food and prepare it; ability to choose the right kind of clothes and take care of them; ability to take care of a home; and ability to take care of children. The boys must acquire ability to use and take care of simple tools, ability to make minor repairs on household plumbing, ability to repair simple electrical equipment, and ability to repair furniture. All are required to learn how to keep clean and neat and use good manners.

Miss Elsa Bauer, chairman of the committee that made the announcement, said, "These embrace the skills and information necessary to be a good citizen, to earn an adequate living, to make a good home, and to maintain good health and contentment." Miss Bauer adds, "For some of the skills designated, the paper-and-pencil test is of questionable value. For these will be substituted statements from authorized persons, such as life guards, Y.M.C.A. directors, and other responsible adults."

You will notice that the object of this interesting educational program is to supply the skills and information necessary to be a good citizen, to earn an adequate living, to make a good home, and to maintain good health and contentment. An educational system that can accomplish these things, and accomplish them in one course, has reason to be proud of itself. The assumption is that if you can take care of yourself in the water, provided you live in a seaport town, if you can fill out application blanks, and make minor repairs on household plumbing, together with a few other matters of similar significance, you will at one stroke have adapted yourself to society and met all your human needs.

The doctrine of immediate needs, or the doctrine of the *ad hoc*, rests on the proposition that individuals need to be able to do things in order to succeed—by the current definition of success—and that societies need to have things done in order to be more successful in the same definition. Individuals and societies need useful things; most of these things are material goods and services.

Hear Harold Benjamin, former Dean of education at the University of Maryland. He says, "Too long Latin has been considered general education and driving a car as special or vocational training. Exactly the reverse is true. Latin is useful only to those students whose needs and abilities require it, while driving a car is useful to everybody." Mr. Benjamin goes on to say that what happened to France after 1939 was a devastating commentary on the French lycée, thus intimating that, if the lycée had offered instruction in automobile driving, the course of history might have been different and that, unless America takes warning by the fate of France and introduces such instruction at once, she may be overtaken by the same fate.

The reverse of this moving appeal by Mr. Benjamin is the story of that Dean of Christ Church who was asked by a student what was the use of studying Greek. The Dean replied, "It is not only the immediate language of the Holy Ghost, but it leads to positions of great dignity and emolument."

In so far as the women's college mentioned, the San Diego High School, Mr. Benjamin, and the Dean of Christ Church are concerned with the needs of students—to behave like mature women, to understand household plumbing, to drive a car, and to achieve positions of dignity and emolument—they are all wrong, though for different reasons. If we can ever find out what the educational system should do, I am sure we shall discover that it will be so difficult as to demand all the time and attention we can give it. It follows that whatever can be learned outside the educational system should be learned outside it, because the educational system has enough to do teaching what can be learned only in the system. The words of Sir Richard Livingstone should be written in letters of fire on every schoolroom wall: "The good schoolmaster is known by the number of valuable subjects he declines to teach." Even if driving a car, understanding plumbing, and behaving like a mature woman are valuable subjects, they can be, and therefore should be, learned outside the educational system.

The study of Greek no longer leads to any positions except positions in the teaching of Greek, which, though of great dignity, are not of great emolument. As identifying a need on the part of the student does not identify a necessity in the curriculum, so identifying a need at one time gives us no assurance that it will continue. If either automobile driving or Greek is to be made a part of the course of study, the argument must rest on something more than that it is or was a need. There are too many needs, too many evanescent needs, too many needs that the educational system cannot effectively cope with.

To refer once more to my favorite women's college, the President told me that it would consume twenty-five years of a student's time to study all the courses offered at his institution. This will suggest the unlimited possibilities of an educational program based on the needs of students. It will also reveal the pitiful plight of the girls, who, on completing their work at this college at the end of two years, must feel that twenty-three twenty-fifths of their needs remain unmet. It seems altogether likely that in this case, as in many others, the college decided that the more courses it could offer, the more students it could attract.

One trouble with the doctrine of needs is the difficulty of identifying a need. How do you know a need when you see one? The usual answer is that you know one by the demand. And the next step is to enlarge your market by the best advertising and sales techniques, through creating a demand for something you could offer to supply. Since the public is likely to have a greater appetite for the *ad hoc*, which can be easily understood, and which, it is hoped, will have immediate practical results, than it has for serious learning, educational institutions that want public support, as all educational institutions in America do, will constantly expand their *ad hoc* activities.

The doctrine of needs thus ends in public relations. I think it fair to say that the dominant concern of school superintendents and university presidents in America is public relations. I have no doubt that the superintendent whose letter I quoted urged indoctrination in the American way of life with a view to ingratiating the school system with the taxpayers, so that, when his plans or expenditures came up for public discussion, he could avail himself of the popularity that his staunch Americanism had won for him. There is not a college or university president in America who would not get rid of what is called big-time intercollegiate football if he felt that it was safe to do so. The howls of the alumni and the public, who have come to rely on his institution to supply them with entertainment on Saturday afternoons in the autumn, ring in his ears as he considers such a decision, and he concludes that it would not be safe.

You know, then, that something is a need because somebody wants it. If the group that wants it is powerful enough, either by reason of its influence or its numbers, to affect your public standing adversely if you do not do what it wants, you do what it wants. Or you try, or, if necessary, pretend, to do what it wants. For many things people want the educational system to do for them it cannot do.

A special problem is created for the American university by the characteristic social, political, and economic organizations of the country, which are known as pressure groups. They have, many of them, the most laudable objects; but their principal object is to get something done. They constantly think of the educational system, and in particular of the universities, as the means through which they can accomplish their desires.

If an occupational group, like the beauticians, for example, wants to combine the high purpose of raising the standards of the occupation with the somewhat different purpose of restricting competition, it will naturally occur to them that the creation of a school for beauticians in the state university, through which all prospective competitors must pass, will limit the number of prospective competitors and enhance the dignity and standing of the occupation. Since almost all occupations in America are organized in this way, and since they all have the same ambitions, there is no end to the creation of new professional schools, as they are euphemistically called, in American universities.

The American universities, because of the influence that these groups may have upon the legislatures that support the state institutions or because of the role that they may be expected to play as donors or fee payers to the private universities, have been unable to resist the claims of these occupational groups. Nor are they able to resist the appeals of industry. The vice-president of a great textile house once described to me his efforts to get some chemical research done by a university department. It was work on a trade secret. He investigated the departments of two or three institutions, only to find that they were allied with his competitors. He finally found a chemistry department in a respectable university that was willing to turn the entire attention of its staff to his problems and not to tell anybody but him the results. "Think of it," he said; "they were willing to do this for $20,000 a year."

Of course, one reason why this chemistry department was willing to do this was that it was not very good. The professors were not intelligent enough to have any problems of their own. But I think the basic reason lies deeper: the American university is supposed to assist in the solution of any current practical problem that anybody has. And when there is money in it, and good public relations in it, the fact that the project runs counter to the purpose of the university, which is to pursue knowledge for its own sake, does not make the lure of such work any easier to resist. The purpose of the university has long since been changed; it is now regarded as a service station for the community. So far have we come from the conception of a university as a center of independent thought.

Let us turn to the basic consequences of the doctrine of needs in education in the West.

One thing, we are told, the democratic citizen in the modern world needs first of all, and that is information. He must have information on every conceivable subject, because his duties as a citizen require him to pass on every conceivable subject. He lives in a world that is being re-made by science and technology. He must know all about them. In America we are reminded that our people have only lately emerged from their isolation to assume a position of world leadership. Americans should know all about Europe, and all about Africa, and all about the Near, Middle, and Far East, as well. Americans should know all about everything.

The first difficulty with this proposition is that current needs and current information simply will not stay current. The rapidity of change in every field today is such that what the father knows of the facts of life is almost useless to his son. Those who painfully acquired information about the Weimar Republic or the Chinese Empire in response to felt needs can feel little need of it now.

The second difficulty with the proposition that everybody has to know all the facts about everything is that there are too many facts. So one of the most

eminent sociologists in America reached the conclusion a few years ago that there were now so many
facts that everybody ought to know that in order to
get time to pour all the facts into the young we should
have to prolong adolescence at least until age 45.
We had, in short, to make a new definition of youth
so that people might learn everything while young.

A final difficulty with the proposition that everybody ought to know all the facts about everything is
that it tends to produce an educational program that
is upside down. If you are going to pour all the facts
about the world into the young, you have to start
early. Yet the one conclusion of Aristotle with which
all educators must agree is that children cannot deal
with the facts of the world about them. Aristotle con-
cluded that in order to understand the facts of life
you have to have experience; these facts cannot be
comprehended by the inexperienced. History, literature, moral and political philosophy, and the social
sciences will not yield up their full lessons to the
immature.

In a country where the people continue their education through their adult lives this difficulty is
troublesome enough. Where there is no serious program of adult education, it takes on more menacing
proportions. There the proposition that everybody
must learn all about everything means that everybody
must learn all about everything while he is in school.
The inevitable result is that the course of study is

jammed with every conceivable subject on the ground that the pupil might find that he needed to know about it, or society might need to have him know about it, in his adult life. The subjects are so numerous that the pupil leaves school without having mastered any of them.

As the doctrine of needs, or of the *ad hoc,* has promoted the disintegration of the program of the schools, so it has promoted the disintegration of the universities. One thing we are all certain of is that society needs specialists and that a man needs to be a specialist if he is to have a successful career. In countries where there is a good basic education this creates no significant problem. The intellectual community rests on this basic education, and specialists can communicate with one another because of the common language, the common stock of ideas, and the common tradition that this basic education has given them. The university of Imperial Germany was an aggregation of specialists. But it would not have been educationally successful or socially tolerable without the humanistic Gymnasium.

The American university as we know it today was founded by men who had studied in Germany and who sought, in the last decades of the last century, to establish the German university in the United States. But they did not import the humanistic Gymnasium. On the contrary, their efforts to build up universities on the German model in the United States succeeded just when the American high school and the American college were beginning to fall apart under the strain imposed upon them by the huge numbers that flocked to them as the twentieth century opened.

The tremendous success, in material, practical terms, that specialism instantly achieved in America led to greater and greater fragmentation of knowledge, with specialists operating in small parts of each fragment. We have now reached the situation where the work of a man in one part of a fragment is incomprehensible to one in another part of the same fragment, to say nothing of a man in another subject. The unity of the modern American university is therefore only geographical, and the topics that can be discussed at the faculty club are the weather and politics, for these are the only subjects the members have in common. When I was on the faculty of Yale, we taught Engineering English in the Engineering School. This meant, of course, that an engineer was taught to talk only to another engineer. Since 50 per cent of the graduates of the Engineering School did not become engineers, I can only assume that they went through life cut off from communication with their fellow countrymen.

All this has had a curious effect on college education in America, which a man begins normally at 18 and completes with the bachelor's degree at 22. It is possible for a boy to receive this degree in many state universities after studying two years of military training, two years of German, physics, chemistry, mathematics, and nothing else. But the inadequacy of his preliminary training and the low standards that he has to meet mean not that he has been well trained in physics, chemistry, mathematics, and German, but that he has not been trained in anything else. Whereas specialization purports to give intensified education in the subject matter of the specialty, what it actually does is to inhibit education outside the specialty.[1]

At the beginning of this century every graduate of a French lycée of a German Gymnasium or an Italian liceo had acquired at the close of 12 years of schooling, at about 18 years of age, approximately as much knowledge of subject matter as three modern college graduates together will have acquired in the United States after 16 years of schooling, at about age 22. If a college student in America specializes in mathematics, he will have arrived at the age of 22 at such branches as differential and integral calculus, analytical geometry, and differential equations. The fundamentals of most of these fields were, however, known to 18-year-old graduates of the old-fashioned European secondary schools, who also knew equally well three other subjects at least: Latin, Greek, and their native tongue.

If a modern American student is graduated from

---

[1] I owe the discussion of this subject to the suggestions of Dr. Hans Elias.

college as a specialist in classical languages at 22, he will not have reached the level that a pupil of an Italian liceo had to reach at about 17. The Italian pupil had to be able by that time to make public, extemporaneous discourses in Latin and to participate in public debates in Latin. And we must remember that these Italian schoolboys knew the calculus as well.

The process of specialization has therefore turned out to be a process of inhibition. The traditional definition of a specialist is that he is a man who learns more and more about less and less In the United States we have discovered that he can be a man who learns less and less about less and less.

These differences between the intellectual accomplishments of American and European students are everywhere admitted in the United States. It is denied, however, that they result from any failure on the part of the American educational system. It is said, first, that America aims to educate everybody, whereas Europe aims to educate the few. It is unfair to compare the attainments of the mass with those of the élite.

It is true that America has up to now undertaken to educate a larger proportion of its youth than any other country in the West. In England today 32 per cent of the children of 14 or over are in school. In the United States the proportion is 76 per cent. In England 20,000 students will enter institutions of higher learning next autumn. In the United States the number is 600,000. We have five times the population and thirty times the number of students above the secondary schools. The difficulties created by the sheer quantity of the American educational enterprise are doubtless very great. Think of the number of teachers that is required. And with that amiable spirit of contradiction characteristic of the Anglo-Saxon race, Americans, who are devoted to education, refuse to pay living wages to their school teachers. The estimate is that 300,000 teachers will quit the profession in the next three years, of whom we shall lose 125,000 this year, not counting those who will die, marry, or retire on account of age. And 10 million more children than are at present in school are expected to enroll by 1960.

The second American comment on the difference between the attainments of American and European students is that the attainments of European students, though interesting, are incomplete, and incomplete in the most important respects. What good does it do the Italian student to be able to make an extemporaneous address in Latin, when he will never feel the need of making one in later life, and would probably not be allowed to make one if he did? What good does it do the graduate of the lycée to know the calculus, if he does not know how to take care of his teeth? What can we expect of a continent in which the young have never been taught how to apply first

aid, take care of themselves in the water, engage
in two or three sports that may carry over into adult
life, write business letters, fill out application blanks,
or budget their incomes, to say nothing of making
minor repairs on household plumbing? No wonder
Europe is impoverished and decadent and America is
rich and powerful.

An American concerned about his country, concerned that her riches and power may be a boon and
not a danger to mankind, may however inquire if it
is altogether clear that the relative poverty and weakness of Europe can result entirely from the intellectual superiority of its educational system. He may
ask whether the huge internal market, the absence of
political subdivisions, the use of a common language,
the tremendous natural resources, and the hitherto
impregnable position of America may not have had as
much to do with the power and riches of the country
as the unusual character of American education. He
may even ask whether it would have been possible
for a country less rich and powerful than America
to survive the educational system that she has.

Such an American may ask, too, whether keeping
everybody in school longer than any other country
necessarily means that everybody in America is better
educated than the mass of the population in any
other country. He may ask whether the American
educational system actually does adjust the young to
their environment or meet the needs of the individual

and of society. In particular he may be permitted
to doubt whether the effort to fit the young into
their current surroundings and to teach them to solve
current problems will equip them with that intellectual power which will enable them to meet new
situations and solve new problems as they arise.
It would appear that, with the extraordinary fluidity
of American society and the drastic changes that
have occurred and are occurring in America's relations with the rest of the world, the intellectual
powers that go by the names of understanding and
judgment are the prime requisite of the American
citizen.

Perhaps the greatest idea that America has given
the world is the idea of education for all. The world
is entitled to know whether this idea means that
everybody can be educated, or only that everybody
must go to school. If education is to be nothing but
a housing project, then we can understand why the
hopes the nineteenth century had of it have not been
fulfilled: the nineteenth century was afflicted with a
delusion; it was off in pursuit of an impractical ideal.
If the education of the whole population is impossible, the sooner we abandon the ideal the better.

To these questions, what education is and who can
and should be educated, I shall revert at a later time.
But I cannot conclude this discussion of the doctrine
of needs, or of the *ad hoc*, without indicating its
significance for the majority of the population of the

world today. They are the peoples of the so-called underdeveloped countries. They are lacking in what the West regards as the indispensable requirements of life, not of civilized life, but of life itself. Their needs are great and pitiful; they need everything. First of all they need useful things, material goods and services.

It is now widely believed that the West should help them get these things, and with this conclusion anybody with a spark of human feeling must agree. At the same time the question arises whether helping them get these things, and doing nothing more, will have the results that are universally anticipated. The general expectation is that, if they have food, clothing, shelter, and adequate sanitation and are assisted on the road to industrialization, they will be happy, or at least happier than they were before. In America it is felt that if they have these things they will line up on the side of the West in the cold war.

In the first place, this theory seems to come close to the Marxian fallacy that the character and conduct of men are determined by the conditions of production. Nothing in history suggests that prosperous nations are less warlike than impoverished ones. Nothing suggests that industrialized countries are less revolutionary than agricultural ones. The people of underdeveloped countries need material goods because they are unable to realize their potentialities as men at their present level of life. We should help them for

this reason and not because we expect them to behave as we would like them to behave.

Another Marxian fallacy is that when the economic problem has been solved, when the classless
society has been achieved, peace will reign and men
will change from voracious animals into angels. All
experience with classless societies, such as universities and monasteries, where the economic differences
among the members are slight and no one is exploit-
ing anybody else in the Marxian sense, shows that
Marx's expectations of peace in the classless society
were bound to be disappointed.

Supplying the peoples of underdeveloped countries
with the means of economic development is a much
more complicated subject than is commonly assumed.
Recent reports on cotton farming in Syria suggest
that the result of mechanization in this field is that the
rich are getting richer and the poor poorer. The
reason of course is that only the rich can afford the
expensive equipment that large-scale irrigation demands. If we are going to be of real help to underdeveloped countries, something beyond the provision
of material assistance is needed, principally a sense,
on our part, of what a just society is and a willingness
to face the disagreeable consequences of joining with
the downtrodden to obtain justice for them at the
hands of the dominant members of the community.
The billions wasted in China should warn us of

the consequences of assisting the corrupt rulers of an unjust society.

The industrial revolution in Japan occurred overnight. Much help came from the West to make the change possible. Educational advisers went out from America. The ruling classes of Japan absorbed the technology of the West to become richer, more powerful, and more bellicose than they had been before. The common people became poorer, weaker, and more insignificant than ever. The two great convictions of modern man, that all problems can be solved by production and education, were shown once more to be illusions. We saw again that production can increase poverty and that education can increase ignorance. The case of the much-vaunted literacy of the Japanese provides striking confirmation of the conclusions of Toynbee and Huxley that the spread of universal, free, compulsory education has promoted the degradation and enslavement of men.

The education that is now proposed for underdeveloped countries, apart from technical training, looks toward the abolition of illiteracy. But of course the question is, what will illiterates read when they have become literate? Do we know it would be an advantage to have people able to read *Mein Kampf*, if they read nothing but *Mein Kampf*? Are we even sure that it is an advantage to have young people able to read comic books, which I take to be the principal cultural manifestation in America in our time?

We cannot even be certain that extensive schooling will actually wipe out illiteracy. The high literacy rate of the Japanese was largely a fiction, and it has been estimated that 50 per cent of the male population of the Chicago high schools are functionally illiterate, that is, they can read letters, or even words; but they cannot tell you what they mean. At best, literacy is a power like any other. It is neutral, like atomic energy; it can be used for evil as well as for good. To assume that everybody will be peaceful and happy if everybody has gone to school or learned to read is as foolish as it is to assume that everybody will be peaceful and happy if the world is industrialized.

I am in favor of material goods, which are undoubtedly goods, of literacy, schooling, and even, within limits, of industrialization. I merely point out that if, in dealing with underdeveloped countries, we are so carried away by the doctrine of immediate needs, the doctrine of the *ad hoc*, that we look only to these immediate needs, the last state of the underdeveloped countries and of the world will be no better, and may well be worse, than the first. The problem is how to help these countries meet their immediate needs and at the same time lay the foundations for a better society and a better world.

We cannot accomplish this if we look for guidance in education to the doctrine of immediate needs. The needs we are seeking to meet are not immediate.

The doctrine of immediate needs provides us with no standards. It gives us no values. It leads us to determine the content of education in terms of the pressures operative in the society. Any connection between these pressures and what is good for the society can at best be coincidental. In the effort to discover how education can help to produce a better society we must turn next to the doctrine of social reform.

CHAPTER III

SOCIAL REFORM AND THE ABANDONMENT OF THEORY

UNDERNEATH the writings of almost all writers on education lies the doctrine of social reform. They cannot look at the society around them and like it. How is the society to be changed? There are only two ways: revolution and education.

Writers on education are not men of action, still less of blood. They shrink from the havoc of revolution. They dream of carrying through the social changes they desire by means of the peaceful process of instruction.

T. S. Eliot's chief complaint of other writers on education is that they seek to use the schools to achieve the social purposes they have at heart. This, he says, is not education, but something else. Then he falls into the pit he has digged for others; he wants to use the schools to advance social purposes of his own. Mr. Eliot wants a society that has both the class, those who have inherited advantages, and the élite, those who have ability, but who may be without inherited advantages. And so, after anathematizing writers on education who seek to obtain the society they desire through the schools, Mr. Eliot says, "Education should help to preserve the class and select the élite." Since this would be bringing about a social change that Mr. Eliot has at heart, it would not, according to his criticism of others, be education, but something else.

The most influential American writer on education, and the most influential American philosopher, is John Dewey. He re-made the American educational system in forty years. He was first of all a social reformer. But his aims were almost exactly opposite to those of Mr. Eliot. He had no objection to the élite; but he was against the class. To him inherited advantages were unmerited advantages. He was an egalitarian.

These examples raise the first question in regard to the doctrine of social reform, which is this: is it possible to achieve the social purposes one has at heart, is it possible to put over a program of social reform, through the educational system? Every society hopes that its educational system will in some way bring the next generation somewhat closer to achieving some of the society's ideals, those in particular which may be approximated without damage, or with imperceptible damage, to the vested interests in the society, that is, without revolution.

But suppose that the ideals of the social reformer are different from those of the society. When Plato planned his ideal state, he did not propose to start it through education, but to perpetuate it that way. His utopia was to come into being through a miracle, which he properly doubted could ever take place. John Dewey on the other hand succeeded, I think, because the social ideals that he favored were those generally popular in the United States.

One of Mr. Dewey's followers, who has invented an educational philosophy called reconstructionalism, wants to use the schools to reconstruct society, and, in particular to bring about world government. I am in favor of world government, and of most of the other social aims that reconstructionalism proposes; but I do not see how the schools can preach world government unless the American people are willing to have this aim promoted in the schools. At the moment I do not believe they are. The proponents of reconstructionalism must first preach to the people. It is as unlikely that world government can be presented as a program in the American schools as that western democracy can be taught as a program in Soviet Russia. A revolution cannot be brought about through the conscious inculcation of revolutionary doctrine in the schools. I am inclined to agree with Mr. Eliot that, if it could be, this would not be education, but something else.

The doctrine of social reform is substantially identical in its results with the doctrine of adaptation and the doctrine of immediate needs. The social reformer is limited to adapting the rising generation to social changes already agreed upon. He is limited to meeting needs that are sanctioned by the society. He can hope to make himself felt in the educational system only after he has won over the society. I should say that, for example, at this moment Mr. Eliot has little chance of persuading the United Kingdom to favor an educational system that preserves the class. It is abolishing the class as rapidly as possible. Unless Mr. Eliot can arouse the population and change the views of those who dominate the United Kingdom, he cannot hope to achieve the social purposes he has at heart through the schools.

Since the doctrine of social reform has the same results as the doctrine of adaptation and the doctrine of immediate needs, the same objections apply to it as apply to the other two.

One in particular needs to be emphasized, and that is the difficulty that grows out of the accomplishment of a program of social reform. Most of the social objectives of the organizations devoted to the education of adults in Sweden have now been achieved. What are these organizations to do now? They must either disappear or devote themselves to other purposes. But the problem would be much more acute if Sweden had set itself to attain these goals through the schools. The school system cannot disappear when it has reached its social goals. If intemperance or slums are eliminated, is the school system to go on preaching temperance or the elimination of the slums? If it does, the schools are cluttered with archaic lumber. If it does not, what are the schools to do? If they move on to other social problems, they will have educated one generation to solve problems that no longer exist, and will be educating another to solve those which may not exist when the pupils have left school.

Consider the embarrassment of the movement for the education of adults in England. This movement originated in the demand for social justice, and especially for equality of educational opportunity. Now its objects have been achieved. This is a serious blow to the movement; for it must concede that its aims were too narrow or go out of business. But suppose that this program of social justice had been carried on through the schools. Year after year pupils would have been taught to go out to work for the aims embodied in the Education Act of 1944. How would they feel in 1945? And what would the schools do after 1944?

But I believe that it is dangerous as well as futile to regard the educational system as a means of getting a program of social reform adopted. If one admits the possibility of obtaining through the schools social reforms that one likes, one must also admit the possibility of obtaining social reforms that one dislikes. What happens will depend on the popularity of various reformers, the plausibility of their causes, and the pressure they are able to exert on the educational system.

Am I saying, then, that the educational system cannot participate in the improvement of society? Not at all. I am saying that it is unwise and dangerous to look at the system as Mr. Dewey, the reconstructionalists, and sometimes Mr. Eliot look at it, as an engine of social reform. I take the view that the object of education is the improvement of society. But to make this view effective you have to know what improvement is, and you have to recognize the limitations, as well as the possibilities, of education. Mr. Dewey, the reconstructionalists, and Mr. Eliot have a faulty conception of improvement. As a result they have a faulty conception of education. Mr. Dewey and the reconstructionalists have not considered the limitations of education. Mr. Eliot has not adequately considered its possibilities.

The failures of which I think they have been guilty result from the defects of their philosophies. Pragmatism, the philosophy of Dewey and his followers, like positivism, the philosophy of Reichenbach and Carnap, is not a philosophy at all, because it supplies no intelligible standard of good or bad. Pragmatism and positivism hold that the only knowledge is scientific knowledge. As the Mad Hatter and the March Hare in *Alice in Wonderland* celebrated unbirthdays, so pragmatism and positivism are unphilosophies. They are even anti-philosophies. Mr. Eliot's philos-

ophy is more subtle and satisfying and exposes him
to less general attack. When he says that education
should help to preserve the class and select the élite,
when, as in *Notes Towards the Definition of Culture*,
he attacks the doctrine of equality of opportunity as
the most mistaken and dangerous dogma put forward
by writers on education, he errs, but he errs in good
company. His views are reminiscent of Aristotle's on
the natural slave. But they are wrong nevertheless.
They reveal a misconception of the nature of man.
Aristotle's views on the natural slave are refuted by a
simple reference to his basic proposition that man is
a political animal. If all men are men, none of them
can by nature be a slave.

These hints may suggest to us the importance of
philosophy in general to the philosophy of education,
a subject to which we shall return. But let us press on
to examine the remaining doctrine that we must re-
view, the doctrine of no doctrine at all.

Thinking is hard work. The development of a coherent philosophy of education, since it carries us
into the formulation of a coherent philosophy in general, is a difficult and ungrateful task. In America the
problems presented by getting everybody into school,
building the schoolhouses to accommodate the vast
hordes who have descended upon the educational
system, and staffing the educational enterprise have
been so serious that American educators may perhaps
be forgiven their reluctance to face the question what

the system is for and how it is to accomplish its purposes. Every time educators address themselves on the subject of education in America, they urge one another to redouble their efforts and forget their aims.

Our conception of the aims of education depends upon our philosophy in general. Philosophy is moribund throughout the world; and Americans are of all peoples the least inclined to philosophize. The most eminent philosophers who have lived in America in the last fifty years were Whitehead and Santayana, who were foreigners, and Dewey, whose philosophy is not, as I have suggested, a philosophy at all.

Besides, American educators have seen the obvious failures that have attended the attempts to build up educational theories. They can see that the doctrines of adaptation, immediate needs, and social reform lead nowhere. Does not this show the futility of trying to formulate a philosophy of education?

Then, too, if we succeeded in building a defensible theory of education, we should have to try to make our practice conform to it, and that might involve the re-education of educators, notoriously the most difficult of all educational tasks, and entrance upon the almost equally difficult program of interesting an entire population in things that ought to interest them, but now do not. If, for example, we decided that, since men are rational animals, they should develop their intellectual powers; and if we decided that all men should develop these powers, we should be required to help all men to acquire the intellectual techniques, such as reading, writing, and figuring, that the use of their intellectual powers demands, and compelled to interest them in ideas and in the intellectual tradition in which they live.

There is also in America a deep underlying conviction that the content of education is irrelevant. Higher education still carries with it a certain social standing, though this is becoming less and less significant as a larger and larger proportion of the population receives university degrees. As Gilbert and Sullivan remarked, when everybody is somebody, nobody is anybody. But, on the principle that what is honored in a country will be cultivated there, education is irrelevant because many of America's most venerated figures, like Edison, Rockefeller, and Ford, had little or none. The works of Horatio Alger, on which the boys of my generation were brought up, all depict an underprivileged lad, who through stalwart character, native shrewdness, and hard work becomes a millionaire. It is true that there is a rumor going around that education may be helpful in making you a millionaire, but, where this is believed, it is taken to mean vocational, not intellectual, education.

But meanwhile we do not know what to do with our children. If we can put them in school and have them stay there until we and the labor unions are ready to have them go to work, we can keep them out of harm's way, or at least out of worse places.

The longer they are in school, the less we shall have
to worry about them.

An imposing Commission of eminent educators
and laymen appointed by the President of the United
States has lately recommended to him that the country look forward to doubling the number of students
beyond the secondary schools by 1960. The basis for
this proposal is the revelation, provided by the Army
General Classification Test in the last war, that at
least 49 per cent of the college-age population has
the ability to complete the first two years of college
work and at least 32 per cent has the ability to
complete additional years of higher education. The
Commission says, "These percentage figures supply
conservative yet conclusive evidence of the social advisability of increased numbers attending college."

These percentage figures supply some evidence
that a larger proportion of the college-age population has the ability to complete certain years of higher
education as it is now carried on. They supply no evidence of the social advisability of having them do so.
The argument that they should do so is based on the
proposition that they have as much ability as those
who are in college now. To know whether it is socially desirable to have them go to college, we should
have to know whether it is socially desirable for all
those who are in college now to be there, a question
on which the Commission offers no evidence, and we
should have to know why those who are not in col-

lege are not there. For example, it does not seem self-evident that a young man of 20 should be in higher education if he prefers to be somewhere else.

The Commission does not seem to care, still less to know, what these young people are to do in college when they get there. The education favored by the Commission is described in words so large and contradictory as to be meaningless. It wants an education "which is not only general and liberal, not only sufficiently vocational, not only for broad competence in citizenship and in the wide use of leisure, but also an integrated and meaningful combination of all these aims at successive levels of education in accordance with the potentialities of each." Such a summary I take to be a statement of the doctrine of no doctrine at all.

This impression is borne out by the more specific recommendations of the Commission, among which are that the colleges should train aviators, insurance salesmen, and photographers; and, if the community is a center for travelers from Latin America, the college should teach Spanish to the taxi-drivers. I am sure that the Commission would have recommended, if it had thought of it, that the college should also teach the taxi-drivers to drive taxis.

When the doctrine of no doctrine at all is in full swing, the educational program that emerges is determined by the tension between the interests of the teachers and those of the taught. Since we do not know what to teach our students, they might as well do what interests them. In many American institutions of higher learning that pride themselves on being progressive, it is now popular to say that there is no curriculum. The President's Commission on Higher Education has this to say of the dark, but unfortunately not distant, future: "As we bring more and more students to the campus, we shall increase in proportion the tremendous variety of human and social needs the college programs must meet. We shall add to the already overwhelming diversity of aptitudes, interests, and levels of attainment that characterize the student body. And so we shall have to increase the diversification of curricular offerings and of teaching methods and materials to correspond."

Since American institutions of higher education are already so diversified that they are split into a million fragments, the Commission's advice is a little like telling a drowning man that he can improve his position by drinking a great deal of water. Its program of infinite diversification rests on a *non sequitur.* Since men are different, the Commission holds that their education must be different. Since there is an infinite variety of individual differences, there must be an infinite variety of educational offerings.

There is no doubt that men are different. But they are also the same. One trouble with education in the West is that it has emphasized those respects in which men are different; this is what excessive specialization means. The purpose of basic education is to bring out our common humanity, a consummation more urgently needed today than at any time in the last five hundred years. To confuse at every point, as the Commission does, the education of our common humanity, which is primary and indispensable, with the education of our individual differences, which is secondary and in many cases unnecessary, is to get bad education at every point. What we have here is a prescription for the disintegration of society through the disintegration of the educational system. This process is now going on in the United States.

The limits imposed on this process are wide. A university student in America may be able to elect almost any courses he chooses; he takes examinations in each of these courses given by the teacher who taught it. When he has taken the required number and passed with the minimum arithmetical average, he is pronounced an educated man. This means that the wise student will study the professor, rather than the subject. He will elect those courses which are the easiest, or which are offered at the most convenient times and places. I once knew a student who boasted that he had graduated from college without taking any course that was offered above the first floor.

Such limits as are imposed on the process are set by the interests of professors. Each professor and each department want the whole time of the student so that he can be thoroughly trained in the professor's or the department's specialty. Since it is obviously impossible for the student's whole time to be spent in this way, the course of study is determined by a process of pulling and hauling and finally emerges as a sort of checkerboard across which the bewildered student moves, absorbing from each square, it is hoped, a little of something that each professor or department has to offer him.

Hence graduation from an American university is no guarantee of literacy. It is no guarantee that the American has any knowledge of the tradition in which, whether he knows it or not, he lives. This tradition is the Graeco-Hebraic tradition. I had a senior of the University of Chicago in one of my seminars who had never heard of Joshua, and not long ago I was interviewed in Paris by a prominent American journalist, a graduate of a great American university who had never heard of Thucydides or the Peloponnesian War.

Hence the failure of communication and community. When I was a student at Yale I could communicate only with those students who had happened, by accident, to elect the same courses that I had elected and whom I happened to know because I sat next to them in the lecture room.

This system deprives the student of one of the greatest contributions that could be made to his education, the contribution of his fellow students. The disintegration of the course of study under the elective system, popularly called the "enrichment of the curriculum," has impoverished the colleges and universities of the United States by depriving them of any common intellectual life. Football and other extracurriculum activities have achieved their exaggerated importance partly because the students have only these activities in common. So an undergraduate of a great American university wrote to the student newspaper not long ago and complained that the curriculum had now reached such richness that one student could not talk to another unless they both happened to remember the score of last Saturday's game.

The doctrine of adaptation, the doctrine of immediate needs, the doctrine of no doctrine at all, and the feeling that the content of education is irrelevant have a common basis. Americans are committed to the proposition that everybody must be educated. At the same time many American educators are convinced that everybody cannot be, in any definition of education that would have been accepted as recently as fifty years ago. At that time it was generally thought that education meant the development of the intellectual powers of men. Many American educators believe that the intellectual powers of most men are so slight that it is not worthwhile to try to develop them. Still everybody must be educated. It is therefore necessary to bring forward a new definition of education, such as that it consists of adjusting the young to their environment or of meeting immediate needs. Or it is necessary to say that the content of education is irrelevant; that having everybody in school is the same thing as educating everybody.

Or to put it another way, the syllogism runs like this: Everybody has a right to education. But only a few are qualified for a good education. Those who are not qualified for a good education must be given a poor education, because everybody has a right to education. Anybody who favors a good education must, therefore, be anti-democratic, because only a few are qualified for a good education, and the true democrat insists on the education of all. The consequence is that those who believe in the capacity of the people are called reactionary and anti-democratic, whereas those who doubt the capacity of the people revel in the name of democrats and liberals.

In the report of the President's Commission on Higher Education, presented by men who have the deepest democratic convictions, we are urged in the name of democracy upon a course that divides the population into the mass and the élite. New institutions, continuing for two years beyond the secondary schools, will be established for the mass, who should not be allowed to clutter up existing institutions, because they are not bright enough. They should attend these colleges, because everybody should go to school as long as possible; but they should not be educated, in any recognizable sense of the word, because they are not capable of it. These new two-year colleges therefore become a kind of gigantic play-room in which the young are detained, or retarded, until we are ready to have them enter upon active life.

Because the concept of education as the development of the intellectual powers of men grew up at a time when society was aristocratic and education was limited to the few, the deeply convinced democrats who wrote the report of the President's Commission assume that anyone who favors an education designed to develop the intellectual powers of men must intend to limit it to the few. They most undemocratically assume that the mass of the people are incapable of achieving such an education. But they have no evidence for this, because the mass of the people have never had the chance to achieve it.

This paradoxical combination of strong faith in the political judgment of the masses with strong doubts of their intellectual capacities has a long history in America. Take the case of Thomas Jefferson. He was a celebrated democrat. He proposed that all children in Virginia should receive three years' free instruction in reading, writing, arithmetic, and geography. He said, "The mass of our citizens may be divided into two classes—the laboring and the learned. . . . At the discharging of the pupils from the elementary schools, the two classes separate—those destined for labor will engage in the business of agriculture, or enter into apprenticeships to such handicraft art as may be their choice; their companions, destined to the pursuits of science, will proceed to the college. . . ."

Three years of free education for all was doubtless a notable contribution to democratic practice in Jefferson's day. But the notion that it is possible to separate human beings at the age of nine or ten into those destined for labor and those destined for learning surpasses the fondest hopes of the psychological testers of our own time and seems to be an oligarchical notion. It seems to be based, not on the differences in the abilities of individuals, but on the differences in their social and economic background. Those destined for labor were destined for it primarily because they were the children of laboring men. Those destined for learning were destined for it because their fathers had wealth and leisure, and it was supposed that they would have them, too. These were the men who were to rule the commonwealth. They, and they alone, needed an intellectual education.

Yet the foundation of democracy is universal suffrage. It makes every man a ruler. If every man is a ruler, every man needs the education that rulers ought to have. If Jefferson did not see this, it may be because in his day the right to vote, and hence to rule, was still regarded as the privilege of the few who had inherited or acquired property. The kind of education we accept now when everybody is destined to rule is fundamentally an extension of the kind that in Jefferson's time was thought suitable for those destined to labor but not to rule. When we talk of our political goals, we admit the right of every man to be a ruler. When we talk of our educational program, we see no inconsistency in saying that only a few have the capacity to get the education that rulers ought to have. Yet the choice before us would seem to be clear: either we should abandon the democratic ideal or we should help every citizen to acquire the education that is appropriate to free men.

CHAPTER IV

THE BASIS OF EDUCATION

THE obvious failures of the doctrines of adaptation, immediate needs, social reform, and of the doctrine that we need no doctrine at all may suggest to us that we require a better definition of education. Let us concede that every society must have some system that attempts to adapt the young to their social and political environment. If the society is bad, in the sense, for example, in which the Nazi state was bad, the system will aim at the same bad ends. To the extent that it makes men bad in order that they may be tractable subjects of a bad state, the system may help to achieve the social ideals of the society. It may be what the society wants; it may even be what the society needs, if it is to perpetuate its form and accomplish its aims. In pragmatic terms, in terms of success in the society, it may be a "good" system.

But it seems to me clearer to say that, though it may be a system of training, or instruction, or adaptation, or meeting immediate needs, it is not a system of education. It seems clearer to say that the purpose of education is to improve men. Any system that tries to make them bad is not education, but something else. If, for example, democracy is the best form of society, a system that adapts the young to it will be an educational system. If despotism is a bad form of society, a system that adapts the young to it will not be an educational system, and the better it succeeds in adapting them the less educational it will be.

Every man has a function as a man. The function of a citizen or a subject may vary from society to society, and the system of training, or adaptation, or instruction, or meeting immediate needs may vary with it. But the function of a man as man is the same in every age and in every society, since it results from his nature as a man. The aim of an educational system is the same in every age and in every society where such a system can exist: it is to improve man as man.

If we are going to talk about improving men and societies, we have to believe that there is some difference between good and bad. This difference must not be, as the positivists think it is, merely conventional. We cannot tell this difference by any examination of the effectiveness of a given program as the pragmatists propose; the time required to estimate these effects is usually too long and the complexity of society is always too great for us to say that the consequences of a given program are altogether clear. We cannot discover the difference between good and bad by going to the laboratory, for men and societies are not laboratory animals. If we believe that there is no truth, there is no knowledge, and there are no values except those which are validated by laboratory experiment, we cannot talk about the improvement of men and societies, for we can have no standard of judging anything that takes place among men or in societies.

Society is to be improved, not by forcing a program of social reform down its throat, through the schools or otherwise, but by the improvement of the individuals who compose it. As Plato said, "Governments reflect human nature. States are not made out of stone or wood, but out of the characters of their citizens: these turn the scale and draw everything after them." The individual is the heart of society.

To talk about making men better we must have some idea of what men are, because if we have none, we can have no idea of what is good or bad for them. If men are brutes like other animals, then there is no reason why they should not be treated like brutes by anybody who can gain power over them. And there is no reason why they should not be trained as brutes are trained. A sound philosophy in general suggests that men are rational, moral, and spiritual beings and that the improvement of men means the fullest development of their rational, moral, and spiritual powers. All men have these powers, and all men should develop them to the fullest extent.

Man is by nature free, and he is by nature social.

To use his freedom rightly he needs discipline. To live in society he needs the moral virtues. Good moral and intellectual habits are required for the fullest development of the nature of man.

To develop fully as a social, political animal man needs participation in his own government. A benevolent despotism will not do. You cannot expect the slave to show the virtues of the free man unless you first set him free. Only democracy, in which all men rule and are ruled in turn for the good life of the whole community, can be an absolutely good form of government.

The community rests on the social nature of men. It requires communication among its members. They do not have to agree with one another; but they must be able to understand one another. And their philosophy in general must supply them with a common purpose and a common concept of man and society adequate to hold the community together. Civilization is the deliberate pursuit of a common ideal. The good society is not just a society we happen to like or to be used to. It is a community of good men.

Education deals with the development of the intellectual powers of men. Their moral and spiritual powers are the sphere of the family and the church. All three agencies must work in harmony; for, though a man has three aspects, he is still one man. But the schools cannot take over the role of the family and the church without promoting the atrophy of those institutions and failing in the task that is proper to the schools.

We cannot talk about the intellectual powers of men, though we can talk about training them, or amusing them, or adapting them, and meeting their immediate needs, unless our philosophy in general tells us that there is knowledge and that there is a difference between true and false. We must believe, too, that there are other means of obtaining knowledge than scientific experimentation. If knowledge can be sought only in the laboratory, many fields in which we thought we had knowledge will offer us nothing but opinion or superstition, and we shall be forced to conclude that we cannot know anything about the most important aspects of man and society. If we are to set about developing the intellectual powers of men through having them acquire knowledge of the most important subjects, we have to begin with the proposition that experimentation and empirical data will be of only limited use to us, contrary to the convictions of many American social scientists, and that philosophy, history, literature, and art give us knowledge, and significant knowledge, on the most significant issues.

If the object of education is the improvement of men, then any system of education that is without values is a contradiction in terms. A system that seeks bad values is bad. A system that denies the existence of values denies the possibility of education. Relativism, scientism, skepticism, and anti-intellectualism, the four horsemen of the philosophical apocalypse, have produced that chaos in education which will end in the disintegration of the West.

The prime object of education is to know what is good for man. It is to know the goods in their order. There is a hierarchy of values. The task of education is to help us understand it, establish it, and live by it. This Aristotle had in mind when he said: "It is not the possessions but the desires of men that must be equalized, and this is impossible unless they have a sufficient education according to the nature of things."

Such an education is far removed from the triviality of that produced by the doctrines of adaptation, of immediate needs, of social reform, or of the doctrine of no doctrine at all. Such an education will not adapt the young to a bad environment, but it will encourage them to make it good. It will not overlook immediate needs, but it will place these needs in their proper relationship to more distant, less tangible, and more important goods. It will be the only effective means of reforming society.

This is the education appropriate to free men. It is liberal education. If all men are to be free, all men must have this education. It makes no difference how they are to earn their living or what their special interests or aptitudes may be. They can learn to make a living, and they can develop their special interests and aptitudes, after they have laid the foundation of free and responsible manhood through liberal education. It will not do to say that they are incapable of such education. This claim is made by those who are too indolent or unconvinced to make the effort to give such education to the masses.

Nor will it do to say that there is not enough time to give everybody a liberal education before he becomes a specialist. In America, at least, the waste and frivolity of the educational system are so great that it would be possible through getting rid of them to give every citizen a liberal education and make him a qualified specialist, too, in less time than is now consumed in turning out uneducated specialists.

A liberal education aims to develop the powers of understanding and judgment. It is impossible that too many people can be educated in this sense, because there cannot be too many people with understanding and judgment. We hear a great deal today about the dangers that will come upon us through the frustration of educated people who have got educated in the expectation that education will get them a better job, and who then fail to get it. But surely this depends on the representations that are made to the young about what education is. If we allow them to believe that education will get them better jobs and encourage them to get educated with this end in view, they are entitled to a sense of frustration if, when they have got the education, they do not get the jobs. But, if we say that they should be educated in order to be men, and that everybody, whether he is a ditch-digger or a bank president, should have this education because he is a man, then the ditch-digger may still feel frustrated, but not because of his education.

Nor is it possible for a person to have too much liberal education, because it is impossible to have too much understanding and judgment. But it is possible to undertake too much in the name of liberal education in youth. The object of liberal education in youth is not to teach the young all they will ever need to know. It is to give them the habits, ideas, and techniques that they need to continue to educate themselves. Thus the object of formal institutional liberal education in youth is to prepare the young to educate themselves throughout their lives.

I would remind you of the impossibility of learning to understand and judge many of the most important things in youth. The judgment and understanding of practical affairs can amount to little in the absence of experience with practical affairs. Subjects that cannot be understood without experience should not be taught to those who are without experience. Or, if these subjects are taught to those who are without experience, it should be clear that these subjects can be taught only by way of introduction and that their value to the student depends on his continuing to study them as he acquires experience. The tragedy in America is that economics, ethics, politics, history, and literature are studied in youth, and seldom studied again. Therefore the graduates of American universities seldom understand them.

This pedagogical principle, that subjects requiring experience can be learned only by the experienced, leads to the conclusion that the most important branch of education is the education of adults. We sometimes seem to think of education as something like the mumps, measles, whooping-cough, or chicken-pox. If a person has had education in childhood, he need not, in fact he cannot, have it again. But the pedagogical principle that the most important things can be learned only in mature life is supported by a sound philosophy in general. Men are rational animals. They achieve their terrestrial felicity by the use of reason. And this means that they have to use it for their entire lives. To say that they should learn only in childhood would mean that they were human only in childhood.

And it would mean that they were unfit to be citizens of a republic.[1] A republic, a true *res publica*, can maintain justice, peace, freedom, and order only by the exercise of intelligence. When we speak of the consent of the governed, we mean, since men are not angels who seek the truth intuitively and do not have to learn it, that every act of assent on the part of the governed is a product of learning. A republic is really a common educational life in process. So

[1] I owe this discussion to the suggestions of Scott Buchanan.

Montesquieu said that, whereas the principle of a monarchy was honor, and the principle of a tyranny was fear, the principle of a republic was education.

Hence the ideal republic is the republic of learning. It is the utopia by which all actual political republics are measured. The goal toward which we started with the Athenians twenty-five centuries ago is an unlimited republic of learning and a world-wide political republic mutually supporting each other.

All men are capable of learning. Learning does not stop as long as a man lives, unless his learning power atrophies because he does not use it. Political freedom cannot endure unless it is accompanied by provision for the unlimited acquisition of knowledge. Truth is not long retained in human affairs without continual learning and relearning. Peace is unlikely unless there are continuous, unlimited opportunities for learning and unless men continuously avail themselves of them. The world of law and justice for which we yearn, the world-wide political republic, cannot be realized without the world-wide republic of learning. The civilization we seek will be achieved when all men are citizens of the world republic of law and justice and of the republic of learning all their lives long.

CHAPTER V

LIBERAL EDUCATION

As ARISTOTLE remarked, politics is the architectonic science. This is one way of saying that the political philosophy accepted by a state will determine the kind of education it has. It is also a way of saying that the practical political situation in which a state finds itself has an overwhelming effect on its educational system. Plato arrived at his curriculum by asking what made a good man and a good soldier. A discipline was included only if it met both requirements. If, as it is sometimes argued, it is the destiny of the West to go to war with the East, then the educational system of the West will have to be designed with this end in view. Education is a secondary subject.

One difficulty is that we cannot answer any educational question of importance by appealing to the test of experience. The countries of the West appear determined to become industrial, scientific, and democratic. There have never been countries that were industrial, democratic, and scientific before. Entirely apart, therefore, from the usual difficulty of proving anything from history, and entirely apart from the difficulty of showing that any social experiment has succeeded or failed, which results from the inordinate number of variables that is always present, the experience of earlier societies would be of little use to us in solving the present problems of education. Even if we knew what their experience showed, it would be almost irrelevant now.

And yet there has always been an education that has been regarded as the best for the best. It has been regarded as the education for those who were to rule the state and for those who had leisure. Unless experimental science has made all the difference, it would seem that some light might be obtained by asking whether and to what degree the education that has always been regarded as the best for the best is still good for them or for anybody else.

How much difference can experimental science make? If it is true that the truth can be discovered only in the laboratory, then we can know very little indeed about education; for we cannot know even whether the statement is true that truth can be discovered only in the laboratory. The truth of that statement cannot be and has not been proved in the laboratory. The questions that science can answer are questions of fact about the physical world. They deal with the material conditions of existence. What is called social science cannot tell us what kind of society we ought to aim at. It is doubtful whether it can even tell us what the consequences of a given social policy will be. The reason, again, is the enormous number of variables that enter into any social situation. I do not deprecate the efforts of social scientists to understand society. I would merely indicate the limits of their disciplines. The great successes of physical science should not blind us to its limitations, either. We can learn from science and technology how to build a bridge. We may, perhaps, learn from social science what some of the social, political, and economic consequences of building the bridge will be. But whether those consequences are good or bad is not a question in either physical or social science.

And so it is of all the most important questions of human existence. What is a good life? What is a good society? What is the nature and destiny of man? These questions and others like them are not susceptible of scientific investigation. On some aspects of them science can shed some light, and such light should be welcomed. But these questions do not yield to scientific inquiry. Nor do they become nonsense, as the logical positivists would have us believe, because they are not scientific.

Here we see again that education is a secondary subject, depending in this case upon philosophy. If there is no knowledge except scientific knowledge, if one object of education is to communicate knowledge, then the object cannot be achieved except through education in science. Unfortunately, the question whether there is knowledge other than sci-

entific knowledge is one that science can never answer. It is a philosophical question.

If the rise of experimental science does not change
the educational situation beyond adding new and
most important branches of knowledge, does the rise
of industry and democracy change it? It certainly
does change it in very significant respects. But does
it change it in the respect in which we are now interested, in respect to content? Let us look at the education that has been regarded as the best for the best
and ask ourselves whether this is still the education
that states the ideal, to what extent it is the best
today, and to what extent it may be usefully offered
to those who were not regarded as the best when this
education was developed.

In the West this education has gone by the name
of liberal education. It has consisted of the liberal
arts, the arts of reading, writing, listening, speaking,
and figuring, and of the intellectual and artistic
tradition that we inherit. It was designed for those
who were to rule the commonwealth, and for those
who had leisure. It has always been thought that
those who could profit by it were a small fraction of
the population. It has never been denied, as far as I
know, that it was the best education for the best.
The question I wish to raise is first, whether it actually was the best education, and second whether it
is so today, and for whom.

For reasons I have already given, I cannot prove

that this education was the best. I cannot prove it
in any scientific way. It is dangerous to try to prove
it by the quality of the men it produced. Who knows
that it produced the men? So it is dangerous for a
university president to boast about his distinguished
alumni. If he is entitled to credit for them, he must
also take the responsibility for those who go to the
penitentiary. I can appeal to the common opinion of
mankind; but mankind could have been wrong. I
think it enough to show that this education was characteristically human and that it was characteristically
western. When I say that it was characteristically
human, I am saying once more that education is a
dependent subject; for what I mean is, of course,
that liberal education conformed to an idea of man
that I regard as sound. This is the conception of
man as a rational animal, an animal who seeks and
attains his highest felicity through the exercise and
perfection of his reason. It is impossible to avoid
being a liberal artist; for a man cannot choose
whether he will be human or not. He can make the
choice only between being a good liberal artist or
a poor one.

Liberal education was characteristically western,
because it assumed that everything was to be discussed. Liberal education aimed at the continuation
of the dialogue that was the heart of western civilization. Western civilization is the civilization of the
dialogue. It is the civilization of the Logos. Liberal

education made the student a participant in the Great Conversation that began with the dawn of history and continues at the present day. Great as other civilizations have been in other respects, no other civilization has been as great as this one in this respect.

Such an education can be called a good education, relative to the conditions under which it developed and flourished. But can it be called nothing more than that? Must we say that industrialism and democracy mean that some other education should now supplant it? We know that this education has already been supplanted in the United States.

By the end of the nineteenth century liberal education in the United States was largely in the hands of the teachers of Greek and Latin. A liberal education was a classical education. The teachers of the classics devoted themselves for the most part to instruction in the languages. It was possible to spend years in the study of the Greek and Latin writers without discovering that they had any ideas. The teachers of Greek and Latin were not interested in ideas. They were drillmasters. The languages in which they gave instruction were required for graduation from all respectable colleges, from all preparatory schools, and even from some public high schools.

In the first twenty-five years of this century the flood overwhelmed the high schools and colleges of the United States. Neither the students nor their parents were prepared to believe that what the classical drillmasters were doing was of any importance. And it must be admitted that the students and their parents were largely right. The classical drillmasters did not reform. They did not insist upon the importance of the classical heritage to modern western man. They were, as I have said, not much interested in that. Instead they insisted that their courses continue to be required. By 1925 the flood swept them away. It was characteristic that in the final battle at Yale, at which I was present, the issue was not about liberal education, or about the importance of the classical heritage, but only about whether one year of Latin should be required for the degree of Bachelor of Arts.

The Twentieth Century was right about the classical drillmasters. It was wrong about liberal education. And it was certainly wrong about what it substituted for liberal education. It substituted for it an infinite, incoherent proliferation of courses largely vocational in aim.

Liberal education consists of training in the liberal arts and of understanding the leading ideas that have animated mankind. It aims to help the human being learn to think for himself, to develop his highest human powers. As I have said, it has never been denied that this education was the best for the best. It must still be the best for the best unless modern times, industry, science, and democracy have made it irrelevant. The social, political, and economic changes that have occurred have not required that liberal education be abandoned. How could they? It is still necessary to try to be human; in fact it is more necessary, as well as more difficult, than ever.

Liberal education was the education of rulers. It was the education of those who had leisure. Democracy and industry, far from making liberal education irrelevant, make it indispensable and possible for all the people. Democracy makes every man a ruler, for the heart of democracy is universal suffrage. If liberal education is the education that rulers ought to have, and this I say has never been denied, then every ruler, that is every citizen, should have a liberal education. If industry is to give everybody leisure, and if leisure, as history suggests, tends to be degrading and dangerous unless it is intelligently used, then everybody should have the education that fits him to use his leisure intelligently, that is, liberal education. If leisure makes liberal education possible, and if industry is to give everybody leisure, then industry makes liberal education possible for everybody.

In most countries, even those in which the education of adults is most highly developed, such education is thought of as compensatory: it makes up for the deficiencies in the formal schooling of the individual. Where formal schooling is vocational, adult education is vocational, too. Where schooling is liberal, as it has largely been in the United Kingdom and Scandinavia, adult education is liberal; for it is thought unjust and undesirable that those who because of the accidents of youth could not complete the formal schooling that the average citizen obtained in childhood and youth should remain without it all their lives.

But this surely is too limited a view of the education of adults. That education should be liberal, and it should be interminable. We are led to this conclusion by looking at the nature of man and the nature of knowledge. The man who stops learning is as good as dead, and the conditions of modern industrial society, which put little strain on a man's intelligence in the conduct of his work, place a premium on the premature cessation of thought. It is impossible to say that a man can develop his highest powers once and for all in youth. He has to keep on using them. I am not suggesting that he must go to school all his life. But I am proposing that he should learn all his life; and I think he will find that informal association with others who have the same purpose in view will help him and them to achieve it.

At a time when only the few were governors and only the few had leisure, liberal education was the education of the few. It has never been anything else. I hope I have shown that the experience of the United States does not prove that liberal education for all is impossible. I cannot refer to any experience to show that it is possible. I am sure that it is difficult.

Aristotle remarked that learning is accompanied by pain. One reason why the philosophy of John Dewey as distorted by his followers remade American education in forty years is that the education it was thought to propose was relatively painless, both for the pupils and the teachers. The principal reason for the popularity in the United States of what is called Progressive Education, in which Mr. Dewey also had a hand, is that the children have a good time in school. In a child-centered society, like that of the United States, any effort to insist on painful work in school naturally encounters resistance.

I must admit also that where pragmatism and positivism hold sway, as they do in most of the West today, anything that I should regard as liberal education may be almost if not quite impossible. So it is impossible where Marxism is the dominant philosophy, and for many of the same reasons. I do not wish to resort to the doctrine of guilt by association in lumping pragmatism, positivism, and Marxism together. But they have at least these characteristics in common, characteristics that are fatal to liberal education in any definition of it that I can comprehend. They all repudiate the past. They all exaggerate the role of science and the scientific method, and appear to hold that the only way of obtaining valid knowledge is the way of experimental science. This of course reinforces the repudiation of the past, because experimental science is a recent phenomenon.

Since the content of liberal education is the greatest ideas that the greatest men have had, regardless of the time at which they lived or the kind of society they lived in, and since the methods of liberal education include the methods of history, philosophy, and language as well as of science, liberal education can hardly arise in the face of pragmatism, positivism, or Marxism. Education is a secondary, dependent subject.

As to pragmatism, positivism, and Marxism, we may hope that they will gradually lose their power and that we may pass on to a coherent view of man as an intellectual, moral, spiritual being. Only if we get our philosophy straight can we think straight about education.

It will be said at once that even with a perfectly straight philosophy there are certain things we cannot do. We cannot make silk purses out of sows' ears, and the more accurately we think about the nature and potentialities of silk, purses, sows, and ears, the more clearly we shall see the impossibility of this task. And we may be told that even if the ears of certain sows are of a texture and consistency that seem to lend themselves to our experiment, the wide variations in the total volume of ears are such that to try to put them all through our silk purse factory on the same machinery will ruin all the ears without giving us any purses.

It is certainly one answer to this to say, as Stringfellow Barr once said, that he was not interested in a silk purse; all he wanted was a good, useful leather wallet. When I urge liberal education for all, I am not suggesting that all the people must become great philosophers, historians, scientists, or artists. I am saying that they should know how to read, write, and figure and that they should understand the great philosophers, historians, scientists, and artists. This does not seem to me an unattainable goal. If it is, unless some better kind of liberal education can be invented than the one that I have described, we shall be forced to abandon universal suffrage; for I do not believe that men can solve the problems raised by their own aggregation unless they can learn to think for themselves about the fundamental issues of human life and organized society. If anybody knows a better way of helping them learn to think for themselves about these issues, I hope he will present it. It seems to me that we must agree at least on this: the alternatives are democracy, with liberal education for all, and aristocracy, with liberal education for the few. If we choose the latter alternative, as Plato did, we may ignore, as Plato did, the education of the masses. All the educational system has to do with them is to find some innocuous way in which they can put in their time until we are ready to have them go to work.

Since education in the West is built very largely on the doctrine of individual differences, so that the study of the individual child and his individual interests is supposed to be the principal preoccupation of his teachers from his earliest days, and premature and excessive specialization is a common characteristic of both the American college and the British public school, it will be argued that a program of liberal education for all ignores the most important thing about men, and that is that they are different. I do not ignore it; I deny it. I do not deny the fact of individual differences; I deny that it is the most important fact about men or the one on which an educational system should be erected.

Men are different. They are also the same. And at least in the present state of civilization the respects in which they are the same are more important than those in which they are different. Politics, the architectonic science, teaches us that we are remorselessly headed toward the unification of the world. The only question is whether that unification will be achieved by conquest or consent. The most pressing task of men everywhere is to see to it that this consummation is achieved by consent. And this can be done only by the unremitting effort to move toward world community and world organization. The liberal arts are the arts of communication. The great productions of the human mind are the common heritage of all mankind. They supply the framework through which we understand one another and without which all factual data and area studies and exchanges of persons among countries are trivial and futile. They

are the voices in the Great Conversation that consti-
tutes the civilization of the dialogue.

Now, if ever, we need an education that is designed
to bring out our common humanity rather than to
indulge our individuality. Our individual differences
mean that our individual development must vary.
If we all struggle to make the most of our individual
human powers, the results will be different, because
our powers differ. But the difference is one of degree,
and not of kind. In a modern, industrial, scientific
democracy every man has the responsibility of a
ruler and every man has the leisure to make the most
of himself. What the modern, industrial, scientific
democracy requires is wisdom. The aim of liberal
education is wisdom. Every man has the duty and
every man must have the chance to become as wise
as he can.

We are living through one of the greatest revolutionary periods in history. Although it is easy to say
that the aims of the revolution on which the majority
of mankind is now embarked are enrichment and
national independence, I am sure that this is a super-
ficial view of the case. The real goal is justice. It
is to throw off the yoke of the oppressor, foreign
or domestic, and to enable every human being, regardless of the accidents of color, birth, or station,
to achieve his highest potentialities. The appeal of
Communism does not lie in any of the theories of
Karl Marx, the fallacies of which can easily be

demonstrated. It lies where his strength has always
lain, in the call for economic justice. Join us, the
Communists say, and you will have all the material
goods of the West without slums, without bloody
warfare between capital and labor, without racial
discrimination, without the criminal, gross brutality
that Marx saw in British nineteenth-century cap-
italism and that everybody can see in its evolution
everywhere. The reply that this economic justice can
be obtained according to Communist ideas only at the
sacrifice of political justice and freedom is meaningless to those who have never known political justice
and freedom or who are not convinced that the
West has achieved political justice or that it fully
understands freedom.

The world is changing very fast, and our ideas are
changing with it. No one except Dr. Malan would
now argue that the white race has a duty to manage
the colored races. No one would suggest, as Abra-
ham Lincoln did, that whites and blacks should not
live together. No one would propose that the underdeveloped countries should not be developed. The
day of the pro-consul is over. The end of colonialism
is at hand.

Since education is a secondary, dependent subject,
as ideas change, the idea of education changes with
them. No man can mourn the death of many ancient
educational prejudices. The notion one encounters in
the East that the aim of education is to raise the

educated beyond the contamination of manual labor, or labor of any kind, is going and must go if the peoples of Asia are to struggle upward to the point where the masses can live human lives. It should not be supplanted by the notion that the aim of education is to learn a trade and get rich on the American plan.

Nor should the West deceive itself into thinking that the industrialization of the world and an increase in its productive capacity can alone set us on the path to peace. The desire for material goods is insatiable. If our educational effort is directed chiefly to increasing the supply of material goods, we shall awaken to discover that we do not know what to do with them. We shall find ourselves in the position of the Sheik of Kuweit, who has 177,000 subjects and an income of $250,000,000 a year. Consider the problem of the United States. What shall it do with its productive capacity? It can divert it, by spending it on arms. It can destroy it, by going to war. Or it can reduce it to absurdity, in capitalistic terms, by giving the goods away or giving other people the money to buy them. There is no reason to suppose that we can solve such a problem by giving everybody vocational training, or that when the problem has arisen on a world scale it can be dealt with by technicians and engineers. Civilization is the deliberate pursuit of a common ideal. Education is the deliberate attempt to form men in terms of an ideal.

A materialistic civilization cannot last. An education that attempts to form men in terms of a materialistic ideal cannot save them or their civilization.

The strand in the civilization of the West that has saved it from materialism and its consequences is the tradition of free inquiry. It is this that has made it possible to say that western civilization is the civilization of the Logos. Liberal education, up to the end of the twentieth century, carried forward the Great Conversation. The collapse of liberal education in the United States has taken us into the doctrines of immediate needs and adjustment to the environment, and has ended in the concept of the educational system as a gigantic play-pen in which the young are to amuse themselves until we are ready to have them do something serious. This concept deprives free inquiry of its justification, threatens academic freedom, and puts the educational system at the mercy of any individual or organization that confuses patriotism with conformity. A year or so ago I talked with a distinguished doctor from Los Angeles about the attempt of the Board of Regents of the University of California to extort an illegal and unconstitutional oath of loyalty from the faculty of that great institution. "Yes, but," he said, "if we are going to hire these people to look after our children we are entitled to know what their opinions are." I think it is clear that the collapse of liberal education in the United States is related as cause or effect **or both** to the notion that professors are people who are hired to look after children.

Our task in North America, where we are the proud and prosperous inheritors of the great tradition of the West, is not performed by making this continent the arsenal, or the granary, or the powerhouse of the world. Our task is to preserve and develop the civilization of the Logos for all mankind.

CHAPTER VI

THE UNIVERSITY

THE continuous lifelong liberal education that makes a man a citizen of the world republic of learning and that is indispensable if he is to do his part to bring about the world republic of law and justice is an intellectual discipline that fits a man to solve new problems as they arise, to grasp new facts as they appear, to meet new needs as they present themselves, and to remould the environment to make it conform to the aspirations of the human spirit.

The pedagogical content of this education may be simply stated. The liberally educated man must know how to read, write, and figure. He must know and understand the ideas that have animated mankind. He must comprehend the tradition in which he lives. He must be able to communicate with his fellow-men. Through familiarity with the best models he must have constantly before him that habitual vision of greatness without which, Whitehead said, any true education is impossible.

The process of such an education should be dialectical. The liberally educated man should be able to continue the Great Conversation that began in the dawn of history, that goes on at the present day, and that is best exemplified by the Socratic dialogue.

Socrates collected opinions, asked questions, clarified terms and ideas, and indicated commitments. That is all he did. All that was required of those who took part with him was that they should try to think and to understand one another. They did not have to agree with Socrates, before or after. They did not have to agree among themselves. If they came to conviction, they did so by their own free will. The only constraint upon them was the law of contradiction. They could not answer Yes and No to the same question at the same time.

As a sound philosophy in general teaches us that men are rational beings, so the educational philosophy dependent on it tells us that though men can be assisted to learn, they can learn only by themselves. They cannot be indoctrinated without violation of the laws of their nature. Criticism, discussion, question, debate—these, are the truly human methods of instruction. Teaching, like midwifery, is a cooperative art. The great truth that Plato presented, somewhat romantically, in the dialogue called the *Meno*, as the doctrine of reminiscence, is that intellectual progress does not take place when the teacher is laying down the law and the pupil is memorizing it, but when teacher and pupil are working together to bring the pupil to the rational answer to the question before him. The Socratic dialogue is the great mirror of pedagogy, whether the student is a child or an adult.

The Socratic dialogue, too, may provide us with a model for the university, the institution that stands at the apex of the educational system and that eventually determines the character of all the rest of it.

In a paper written for the tercentenary of Harvard, Alfred North Whitehead said that the task of the universities is intellectual leadership and proposed that Harvard should fashion the mind of the twentieth century as the University of Paris fashioned that of the Middle Ages.

When I read Mr. Whitehead's article, I asked myself whether the universities had ever exerted intellectual leadership or had ever fashioned the mind of any epoch except the Middle Ages. Since the universities were not established till the Middle Ages, they could not have fashioned the mind of the ages before. As to the ages afterward, their minds were fashioned by individual men, or by small groups of men, most of whom were not associated with universities. One of the most striking things about the works that have made the minds of various ages is that almost none of them were written by professors. And where they were written by men who were sheltered by universities, the men and not the universities were responsible. That Newton worked at Cambridge should not blind us to the fact that in his day the British universities were sinking into a deep torpor, probably brought on by port, from which they were not to awaken for more than a hundred and fifty years. The influences that have been most effective on a world scale in fashioning the mind of the twentieth century up to now are Marx, Darwin, and Freud, not Heidelberg, Oxford, or the Sorbonne.

Ever since Mr. Whitehead's article appeared I have been trying to figure out how it was that the universities fashioned the mind of the Middle Ages when they have not been able to do so since. In order to discover whether the universities can exert intellectual leadership again, we have to find out how they did so once. Mr. Whitehead's answer was *suggestiveness.* They did it by suggestiveness, and suggestiveness comes from action. So Mr. Whitehead said that the way Harvard could do for modern times what the University of Paris did for the Middle Ages was to absorb into itself those schools of vocational training for which systematized understanding has importance.

This answer seemed inadequate to me when I first read it and has grown more so with every passing day. If this is all there is to it, the American universities should long since have fashioned the mind of this age, for they have absorbed into themselves not only all those vocational schools for which systematized understanding has importance, but also every other vocational school, so that the ordinary American university presents an array of vocational schools of incredible variety and insignificance.

What is important for us is not the fact that the medieval universities entered into the life of their time, but the way in which they did it. In the Middle Ages the whole university was both speculative and practical. The insight that produced this organization was that everything speculative has significance in the practical dimension, and everything practical, to be worth study, must have a speculative basis. The purpose for which any action was studied or taught was to increase the understanding of that action and what it implied. Not every occupation was a profession in the Middle Ages. A profession was a body of men trained in a subject matter that had intellectual content in its own right. The aim of the group was the common good. The universities of the Middle Ages did not enter into the life of their time through having schools that actually or ostensibly prepared men for vocations, but through a combination of the speculative and the practical that made the two indistinguishable as subjects of study and teaching.

The disciplines of the Middle Ages were studied together because they were lived together, and must be. Professors and students had a common heritage in the tradition of learning. They had a common training in the methods and techniques appropriate to each discipline. They did not necessarily agree on what ideas were basic, but they did have a common acquaintance with the ideas that could seriously claim to be basic and a commensurate ability, derived from a common training, to appraise and understand those ideas. The characteristic intellectual apparatus of the medieval university, as Mill nostalgically points out in his essay *On Liberty*, was the disputation, which has now disappeared from the Anglo-Saxon world.

If it is these features of the medieval university, rather than its specifically vocational interests, that helped the University of Paris to fashion the mind of the Middle Ages, we can understand why no universities since the Middle Ages have been able to duplicate the accomplishments of those which existed then.

In the essay that he wrote for the Harvard tercentenary, Étienne Gilson pointed out that the scholars of the Middle Ages wanted to universalize the faith. They had a strong belief in the universal character of rational truth. "Since faith could not possibly be proved by reason," Mr. Gilson says, "the only hope of universalizing it was to make it acceptable to reason." The method of seeking to make faith acceptable to reason was endless argumentation. Mr. Gilson concludes: "Thus did it come to pass that, viewing themselves as members of the same spiritual family, using a common language to impart to others the same fundamental truth, those medieval scholars succeeded in living and working together for about three centuries, and so long as they did, there was in the world, together with a vivid feeling for the universal character of truth, some sort of Occidental unity."

The end of the Middle Ages brought with it great gains in every field of knowledge, except possibly philosophy and theology. The medieval period had been an age of debate. What followed was age upon age of discovery. Inquiry was promoted by specialization and the experimental method. In the Middle Ages the members of the University of Paris thought together. The subjects that were studied were studied together. Teachers and students tried to see everything in relation to everything else. They had to— their object was understanding through discussion. The discoverer or the experimenter, on the other hand, had to be a specialist as soon as possible; his demands gradually broke down the common training of the medieval period. Since his object was to open new fields, he did not care for the tradition of learning. Descartes, for example, began by repudiating all previous thinkers.

As the specialties multiplied, specialists could not think together. The specialties were too numerous and diverse to be studied together. The discussion that was the principal activity of the medieval university had to stop. The standard by which the medieval university determined what should be studied had to go. Anything that any specialist wanted to study had to be included. Who could say that one vocational school was any more appropriate to a university than any other?

The processes of the last eight hundred years have been favorable to the formal emancipation and education of the people. But in a period of discovery, a period of specialization and esoteric experiment, what can their education be? Almost by definition nobody can know anything except a specialist, and he can know nothing outside his specialty. At the same time all the wonderful things that are happening in science can be made exciting to the people, and a profit is to be garnered by writing them up in a cheerful and inaccurate way for popular consumption.

So Hermann Hesse, in his novel *Magister Ludi*, calls this the "Age of the Digest." This is the period of the fragmentary, the topical, the diverting—the period of the uncomprehended trifle. It is a period of propaganda and publicity.

The most remarkable paradox of our time is that, in proportion as the instruments of communication have increased in number and power, communication has steadily declined. Mutual intelligibility is probably a rarer phenomenon now than at any time in history.

The task of intellectual leadership now is to bring about a genuine communion of minds. But this is still the age of discovery. It is, therefore, still the age of the individual thinker, of the specialist. And, as a consequence, it is the age of the digest, with all the

incoherence and triviality that must characterize such
an age. If there is to be a new cultural epoch and not
simply a further cultural collapse, the distinguishing
feature of the new epoch must be this: it must combine discovery and discussion. The object must be,
while retaining and encouraging the drive toward
discovery, to restore the conditions of conversation.

If then we ask how the university can repeat the
brilliant leadership of the University of Paris, and if
the task of that leadership is to bring about a genuine
communion of minds through the restoration of the
conditions of conversation, we run at once against
the fact that in the speculative realm the modern
university is chaotic, that in the practical realm it is
silent, and that the two realms are sharply divided
from each other. The chaos in the speculative realm
means that ideas are unclear, unrelated, and uncomprehended. The silence in the practical realm means
that on matters of life or death to our society no
disinterested voice reaches the public. The division
of the speculative and the practical impoverishes
both. The conditions of conversation do not exist
within the university. In the academic world there
is no genuine communion of minds.

One of the things most often proposed as a step
toward communion of minds is international co-
operation in science, art, and scholarship. Although
such co-operation should be promoted, it would not
do much to establish a community within a uni-

versity, or within a country, or throughout the world. A scholar in one country can now communicate with another scholar in the same field anywhere in the West. He is usually incapable of communicating with a scholar in another field on his own campus. If the university as such, the university as distinguished from its individual members, is to exert intellectual leadership toward creating a genuine communion of minds, it must first have such communion within itself.

The task of bringing about communion within a modern university can be performed, if it can be performed at all, only through a common training, a common appreciation of the different kinds of knowledge and of the different methods and techniques appropriate to each, and a common, continuous discussion on the Socratic model of those ideas which can pretend to be important, together with the consideration of the practical implications of those ideas.

In such a community, men, even if they disagree, should be able to relate what they are thinking to what others are thinking or have thought on the same point and on all points connected with it. The individual should be able to locate himself in a universe of discourse. Ideally, enough unity should prevail in the world of thought so that no idea, no theory, doctrine, or general view of things could exist in isolation from the rest.

A university should be an intellectual community

in which specialists, discoverers, and experimenters, in addition to their obligation to their specialties, recognize an obligation to talk with and understand one another. If they can restore the conditions of conversation among themselves, they can become a university, a corporate body of thinkers, that can exert intellectual leadership and hope to make some modest efforts to fashion the mind of its time. They could hope to achieve a *Summa Dialectica*, a summation of the possibilities of thought, of the methods of analyzing, relating, and understanding ideas, with an indication of real agreements and disagreements. It may not be possible to reconcile the ideologies that now divide the world. But we cannot tell whether or not they can be reconciled until we have first tried to get them clear.

The problem, then, is to retain the values of the age of discovery, to regain those of the age of debate, and to put an end to the age of the digest. And the problem is to do this through the university as a whole, not through individuals who happen to reside in it. To do this it would have to think as a university, and think both speculatively and practically. The intelligence of the university as such would have to be focused on great speculative and practical issues.

If, then, some modern sage, like Mr. Whitehead, were to ask once more how a university might exert intellectual leadership and fashion the mind of the twentieth century, he might create for himself a sort of myth or dream of the higher learning. In this myth he might fancy that the university, in addition to making the most sensational discoveries in all fields of knowledge, asked itself what were the crucial problems of contemporary civilization upon which the intelligence of the university might shed some light. He might see the university studying such questions as the crisis in our culture, the conflict between East and West, the relations of church and state, or the responsibility of the public for the health of the community, and giving its impartial advice to a people distracted by propaganda. He might imagine that even the specialized, theoretical thought of the university would be enriched and a genuine communion of minds advanced by this effort to focus the intellect of the university upon the continuing problems of human society.

Of course the sage would be enough of a sage to realize that the ideas that were brought to bear upon practical problems could not originate in or be validated by any official creed, dogma, or authority. In his dream the university would be aiming at restoring the conditions of conversation and reinterpreting basic ideas. Thus he would see the university taking up one such idea after another and discussing, clarifying, and modifying it in the light of modern discoveries. He would see the university as a whole, the university as such, moving in both the speculative and the practical orders toward communion, unity, understanding, and the enlightenment of the world.

This is, of course, merely a myth, or a dream. And I fear that it will always remain so. I fear that the university, in Europe as well as in America, is so far sunk in empiricism, specialism, and positivism that we cannot look to it to repeat in our time the brilliant leadership of the University of Paris. What, then, is the world to do for intellectual leadership, which it needs more today than at any time in the past five hundred years?

I suggest that we may require another institution, which would leave the university to go on as it is doing now, which would not supplant the university, but which would take up the burden the university has laid down.

Such an institution would be composed of men who were prepared to conduct a continuous Socratic dialogue on the basic issues of human life. They would be specialists, but they would have passed beyond specialism. They would bring their specialized training and points of view to bear upon the common task of clarification and understanding. They would be prepared to think, both speculatively and practically; they would be able to communicate with one another and with the public. They would retain the advantages of the Age of Discovery and regain those of the Age of Debate.

They would establish a genuine communion of minds. They would know no limitations of national boundaries; for they could be assembled from all parts of the world. They could therefore at once advance and symbolize that world community, that world republic of learning, without which the world republic of law and justice is impossible.

They might give light to the nations now wandering in darkness. They might fashion the mind of the 20th century and make it equal to the dreadful obligations that Providence has laid upon it.

INDEX

Ad hoc, doctrine of, 26-47·
Adjustment (adaptation),
   theory of, 14-25
Adult education, 51-52, 84-85
Alger, Horatio, 56
Alice in Wonderland, 53
Amusement, search for, 19
Aristotle, 35, 54, 72, 77, 86
Army General Classification
   Test, 57
Asia, 44-46, 92
Automobile driving, 28

Barr, Stringfellow, 88
Bauer, Elsa, 27
Benjamin, Harold, 28-29
Buchanan, Scott, 75 n.

California, University of, 93
Cambridge University, 97
Carnap, Rudolf, 53
Chicago, Ill., literacy in high
   schools, 46
Chicago, University of, 11,
   12, 19, 61
China, 44-45
Christ Church, Dean of, 29
Civilization of the Logos, 81,
   93-94

Classical education, 28, 29,
   38-39, 40, 82-83
Classless societies, 44
Clown, and college credit, 13
Cold war, 20, 22, 24, 43
Comic books, 22
Communication, 5-9, 102
Communion of minds, 103-5,
   107-8
Communism, 21, 23, 90-91
Conformity, 20-22, 25
Contradiction, law of, 96
Cosmetology, 16
Criticism, 10-11, 25
Cultivation, mass, 6-10, 14

Darwin, Charles, 98
Debate, age of, 101, 105, 107
Democracy, and education,
   68, 70, 88
Descartes, René, 101
Despotism, 68, 70
Dewey, John, 15, 49, 50, 52,
   55, 86
Digest, age of, 102-3, 105
Discovery, age of, 101-2, 105,
   107
Doctrines, educational, *see*
   Education, doctrines
Don Quixote, 20

109